HAUNTED
POSEY COUNTY

T0274759

JONI MAYHAN

Haunted
America

Published by Haunted America
A Division of The History Press
Charleston, SC
www.historypress.com

Front cover: The Hovey House was home to Governor Alvin P. Hovey, who lived there from 1871 until his death in 1891. The building has had many incarnations over its illustrious history, including being a Masonic temple. It's now used for county offices, but the voices from its past won't be silenced. All photographs by the author unless otherwise noted.

First published 2022

Manufactured in the United States

ISBN 9781467150774

Library of Congress Control Number: 2022937900

CONTENTS

CONTENTS

Acknowledgements

W hen John Rodrigue from The History Press asked me if I'd write a book about the hauntings in Posey County, I hesitated. As the author of twenty-three other books, including *Haunted New Harmony*, which tells the spooky tales of one Posey County town, I knew I could write the book. My hesitation came from my lack of knowledge about the ghosts in the other towns. I had a vague recollection of a few haunted locations but certainly not enough to fill an entire book.

I immediately reached out to Posey County historian Ray Kessler. While he didn't claim to know about any hauntings, he was well versed in the history. As I wrote each chapter, I contacted him for historical information, and he tirelessly provided it. Once, during the middle of a snowstorm, he got in his car and drove to the historical society to find a piece of information I was looking for. His name is all over this book for good reason. I couldn't have done this without you, Ray.

I'm also indebted to Linda Warrum, who is the historian in New Harmony. She dug through boxes and records to help me uncover information that was essential to the integrity of the historical aspects of my beloved town.

Additionally, I'm profoundly thankful to my team of beta readers. These are normal people with a love of reading who weren't afraid to tell me what they thought. Starting this list is fellow author Gare Allen, who read every chapter as I wrote it. Appreciation also goes to Tracy Hoehn for her guidance on commas and for helping me investigate some of these locations. Thank you, Jim Budziszewski and Paula Bundy, for providing me with opinions on the content as well. Every author needs people in her camp who aren't afraid to be honest and upfront, and these people were unwavering in their efforts.

And, of course, thank you to all the people who put fear aside and told me their stories. Without them, this book couldn't have been written.

My family and friends have supported me throughout my entire journey. I would be remiss to not mention them as well. Many thanks to my parents for molding me as a writer and also to all the friends along the way for enhancing my journey.

INTRODUCTION

I've always been fascinated by ghosts. It started when I was a young child, tucked away in my bedroom for the night, watching as shapes separated from the shadows. They approached my bed like night stalkers, moving toward me in slow motion. I never knew if they were malicious or simply curious about this small child who could see them. They frightened me, so I always screamed, causing them to dissipate like smoke as my mother came running into my bedroom.

After I'd been tucked back under my covers with the promise that ghosts didn't exist, they'd chuckle from the shadows, knowing they weren't finished with me. It would start all over again once the hallway light was extinguished.

It never occurred to me that ghosts didn't exist. As someone born with a sixth sense, I felt them lingering even when others did not. I came to fear the darkness, never trusting I was alone within it.

As a child growing up in Posey County, I felt the dead wandering the streets and floating across the wintering fields. I knew which places made me anxious and which ones gave me solace. I never wondered why a midwestern county would be so fraught with ghosts until I moved away and then returned thirty years later.

This time, I wasn't a fearful child who was frightened by shadows; I was a paranormal investigator with more than three hundred investigations under my belt. Instead of hiding from them, I began seeking them out, trying to learn their stories. What I found was interesting.

Hauntings aren't confined to timeworn Gothic mansions. They don't fixate on cemeteries and old battlefields. They are everywhere. They are in random houses in the middle of subdivisions. They are in restaurants, art galleries, libraries and sheriff's departments. There is even one at my local Dollar General.

For most people, this would be surprising. If you drove through southern Indiana, you'd see lush fields laid out like patchwork quilts, small homey towns and a vast sky that seems larger than possible. It would be the last place you'd expect to discover a haunting.

Posey County sprawls out over 420 miles of low, rolling hills, giving way to the flatlands of the river bottoms. It has five towns, ten townships and thirty unincorporated communities, many of them nestled in the fields and forests. Nearly twenty-five thousand people live there now, with many more having died there over the course of our history.

It's a beautiful area of the country. It's a place where you'll see more John Deere tractors than Ferraris, more backyard cookouts than fine dining. People are friendly. They will smile and wave at you even if they don't know you. If you look at a map of Indiana, you will find us at the very tip of the boot, where the two rivers meet.

I've always felt that water is a strong conductor for paranormal activity. The energy and power of the raging water create a perfect situation for holding and maintaining spiritual energy. Is this why Posey County is so haunted?

It might be part of the reason, but it's not the full answer.

Ghosts are everywhere, even in rural communities like Posey County.

PART I

MOUNT VERNON

I stood on the courthouse lawn listening for the cries of the dead. After everything that happened there in 1878, it would stand to reason that the area would be haunted.

In the late 1800s, the river port town of Mount Vernon, Indiana, was still trying to find its identity. It was the largest town in Posey County and was designated as the county seat in 1825. In some ways, it was a riverboat town, as it catered to the barges and boats drifting past on their way to Louisiana. In other ways, it was a farming community with a growing industry and plentiful commerce.

Thirteen years had passed since slavery was abolished, but it was apparent the times were still precarious for a dark-skinned person.

In October 1878, seven African American men were accused of raping three known prostitutes at knife point. By the time the sun set that fateful day, four of the men were dead.

A mob of nearly three hundred men swarmed the courthouse, removing the four men from the jail. They hanged them from nooses on the courthouse square. The other three men were chased down over the course of the next three days and faced horrific deaths. One man was chopped into pieces and stuffed down the courthouse toilet. Another man, who was hiding in a train car, was thrown

The Posey County Courthouse, located in the heart of Mount Vernon, Indiana.

into the coal firebox of the steam engine to be burned alive. The last man was chased down, killed and stuffed into the trunk of a tree.

All seven of the deaths were appalling. I can only imagine the pain and suffering they endured, but as I stood there on the very spot where the men were hanged, I couldn't find a trace of their presence.

I spoke with Judge Jim Redwine, who was a renowned judge for the Circuit Court of Posey County from 1981 until he retired in 2018. Redwine penned the compelling story about the courthouse lynchings in his book *Judge Lynch!* and has been working diligently over the years to encourage the city to erect a monument on the courthouse lawn to pay tribute to the men who lost their lives in the lynching.

While Redwine doesn't necessarily believe in ghosts, he said several of the courthouse employees have felt something eerie in the basement over the years.

In his book *Gavel Gamut Greetings from JPeg Ranch*, he details a story about a man who frequently spent time in the basement going through records. The man, who remained anonymous, said that a dark form passed by him in the southwest corner of the building. Frightened, the man ran up to the County Clerk's Office and told them what he had witnessed. The women working there were nonplussed, telling him, "Oh yeah. We know. We have felt its presence several times. We call him George."

Could it be from the lynchings?

Chances are it came from any number of events that transpired at the courthouse over the years. Sometimes, it's not the big tragedies that inspire a haunting; it's due to the normal, everyday lives that were lived there.

The city of Mount Vernon has endured its fair share of tragedy. Beyond the lynching, there have been murders, fires, epidemics and floods.

According to Ray Kessler, the Posey County historian, "Our community has been touched by many deadly diseases from cholera to Spanish flu and now COVID. Fires have been destructive, and shipwrecks have produced victims and heroes."

"Sometimes evil raises its ugly head with Klan activity and mob injustice. For every southern sympathizer, every Knight of the Golden Circle or White Cap, there is an abolitionist, a philanthropist, a Civil War hospital, volunteers taking in flood victims or a club helping the poor or orphans," he added.

If you go beyond the broad stroke of the city's history and dig deeper into the lives of those who once called Mount Vernon home, you'll see how spiritual unrest could have been created. Take, for example, a man named Harry Long. He was murdered while sitting on his front porch on West Sixth Street by his own cousin, who felt Harry was paying too much attention to his wife. The house he lived and died in still stands. It wouldn't surprise me if the current owners hear phantom footsteps in the wee hours of the morning.

Another example is the two-story brick farmhouse at the edge of town that is haunted by the ghost of a little girl who died of the Spanish flu back in 1918. The owners of the home see her on occasion and keep a selection of toys on hand for her to play with.

The ghosts of the past never truly disappear. They're always there, whether you believe in them or not.

WATER WORKS BUILDING

123 College Street
Mount Vernon, Indiana

A massive amount of history happened on the corner of College Avenue and Water Street. It was a lot to comprehend.

I was early for my meeting with Chuck Grey, the water superintendent for the city of Mount Vernon, so I just stood there and tried to take it all in.

From my vantage point on the corner, I had a clear view of the impressive Ohio River. A tugboat pushed a long, flat barge across the grayish-blue water while children played at the playground on the banks in front of it. Several cars whisked past on their way back from the plastics plant down the street. The wind coming off the river smelled heady but not unpleasant. It was the kind of place where you could stand for hours and watch the world go by.

I love the way history layers on top of itself. If you didn't know the whole story, you'd never realize all of the monumental accomplishments that transpired there. I tried to mentally erase the blacktop streets, the utility poles and the various buildings and imagine what the land looked like before the first settler climbed the bluff and staked claim to the land.

It must have looked like paradise to Andrew McFaddin. He had been out on a hunting trip and happened upon the tall bluff of land by accident in 1795. It didn't take him long to realize it might be a good place to settle. The land was high enough from the river to prevent frequent flooding, and the

The view of the mighty Ohio River from the Water Works Department.

hunting was exceptional. I wondered if he once stood on the same place that I stood, also taking it all in.

He must have liked what he saw, because he built his house there in 1805. It was a simple structure, assembled from trees cleared from the land, but it provided the family with shelter and a place to flourish. The McFaddins lived there for years as the city of Mount Vernon developed around them.

Decades after their homestead was gone, the land was cleared, and a hotel was built on the lot. The only trace that was left of the old McFaddin homestead was a small cemetery at the back corner of the lot where Andrew and four of his family members were laid to rest.

If you stood on that corner during the mid-1800s, the scenery would have looked a bit different. The river port was busy with people coming and going, and the hotel was a popular place to stay. According to Ray Kessler, it also had a colorful history. "The hotel was built by Turner Nelson. It was a fine Georgian structure with a small pillared portico in front and a cupola on top with many small panes of windows. Visitors to our town, usually those with some means, would stay here coming in off the steamboats," he added.

"Meals were served, and usually there was some sort of entertainment. During the cholera epidemic of the 1870s, one infected soul died here. The lady who cleaned the sheets also died, as did people of her family," he said.

Another fascinating tidbit of information revolves around a bear. Apparently, a produce buyer from Tennessee caught a bear cub and gave it to the Nelsons. They raised it as a pet, keeping it chained up in the front yard of the hotel. After it grew to two hundred pounds, it became aggressive and wasn't content with being chained up. The family then slaughtered it and served bear steaks to their guests.

Years later, the Nelson House was sold to U.G. Damron, who became the mayor of Mount Vernon in 1872.

"As it aged, it became a second-rate hotel and finally a tenement house. Like all things, it served its purpose and was torn down. By August 1955, the site became the location of the Water Works Department office," Ray said.

As I stood there on the corner, I tried to wrap my mind around it. The plot of land that had once held the McFaddins' homestead, and later a hotel, was now industrial and purposeful. Tall metal walls rose from the ground, housing the town's water department. The only indicator of the land's history came from two monuments on the property. One was a sign paying tribute to the memory of the McFaddin family, and the other memorialized the first cemetery.

That's where things get intriguing.

It was finally time for my meeting with Chuck Grey. He gave me a tour of the property and told me an interesting story.

"Have you heard about the McFaddin family cemetery?" he asked.

I knew it once existed but didn't know the full story, so he led me around to

the parking lot that separates the Water Works Building from its offices. "See that telephone pole?" he asked me, pointing toward a spot near the entrance to the building. "That's where the cemetery used to sit." He figured out its placement after reviewing old newspaper articles.

It was a bit startling. If there was a cemetery in that spot, there was no trace of it now. It felt a bit sacrilegious to me, and I wondered if the ghosts felt the same way.

According to Chuck, the area was taken over by the Water Works Department in 1955. At that point, the headstones were moved several feet to make room for the building. There are two stories about what happened to the bodies, and no one is certain which story is accurate. Some say that in 1976, a street department employee pushed the headstones into the creek to get them out of the way and

The memorial sign near the Water Works Department paying tribute to Mount Vernon's first cemetery.

Top: In 1934, the City of Mount Vernon also erected a sign memorializing the McFaddin family. This sign sits in front of the Water Works Department.

Bottom: According to Chuck Grey, the original McFaddin Cemetery was located just behind where the truck is parked in this photo.

just left the bodies. Others claim that the bodies were moved to the old McFaddin Cemetery on the outskirts of town.

Chuck was curious about it, so he visited the McFaddin Cemetery, hoping to find the graves. As he walked around, he wasn't sure what to think. The cemetery is filled with McFaddin graves, but none of them are old enough to belong to the original settlers. All he found were five concrete slabs missing the markers. It's possible someone broke them off, but the

McFaddin Cemetery. Notice how McFaddin is spelled differently on this sign. According to Ray Kessler, the Posey County historian, the correct spelling is McFaddin, which is how the family spells it to this day.

names of the people who were buried there are lost and forgotten. While Chuck has spent a fair amount of time trying to find out, the information has remained elusive.

It should surprise no one that upheaving a cemetery could cause a haunting. Combined with the rest of the history, it would be shocking if the area wasn't haunted.

As it turns out, several ghosts still lurk on the property. For many years, people at the Water Works Department have experienced strange happenings. Nearly every person who works there has seen or heard something they can't explain. Some of the occurrences have been explainable, but other encounters have nearly caused people to run from the building. And it seems to happen all around the property.

The smaller building that houses the Water Works Department offices sits across a small parking lot from the main building. The people who work there have experienced their fair share of paranormal activity.

One common occurrence involves a scent. "We smell cigar smoke," one employee told me. "It happens out of the blue. It's so strong, you know exactly what you're smelling," she said. Normally, the odor disappears as quickly as it appeared, leaving them wondering if they imagined it.

Several members of the office staff have also experienced something strange with the adding machine. Without warning, it will start spitting out tape as though invisible hands are pushing the buttons. And if that isn't enough, the ghosts are also prone to jostling the employees. One time, Chuck was in the walk-in safe and felt someone tug on the back of his shirt.

He turned around, fully expecting to find someone standing there, but the room was empty.

The phenomenon is never-ending. If employees aren't smelling strange scents or hearing odd sounds, the doors often open and close in empty rooms. While most people would find it eerie, the people who work there have gotten used to it. It's simply a normal part of the workday.

Chuck then led me into the main building. The first thing you notice when you walk in is the sound. The hum and whirl of machinery fills the air to the point where you need to almost shout to carry on a conversation.

The area has changed a lot over the years. They used to have large pools that filtered the water, but they've been replaced by more modern implementations. That area is now open, with several glass-front offices.

Chuck pointed toward the far end of the building, where the Damron house once stood. "This is where we experience the most activity," he told me.

Sometimes, they smell women's perfume, and he assured me with a chuckle that the smell isn't coming from any of them. Other times, they'll hear whistling, as though someone is walking through the room cheerfully sharing a tune.

When people hear it, they stop what they're doing and look around. It always happens when the building is empty and there's no clear-cut explanation for the sound. They also smell cigar smoke in the main building.

Some of them attribute the smell to a longtime worker named Glen who died there ten years ago. "He was a big cigar smoker, and he always smoked a specific blend called Backwoods Cigars. It smells exactly like that. You always have that history of people who worked here and quit, but we also had guys who worked here for forty years or more, and you get to know them," Chuck said.

Chuck isn't sure where the haunting comes from, but he has several ideas. One of them is a man who actually died on the property. During the Blizzard of '77, he went out to warm up his car after working the second shift. As he sat there in his car, he suffered a fatal heart attack and wasn't found until the next morning. He might very well be one of many souls haunting the building.

Most people believe the majority of the haunting comes from the Damron house. According to rumor, in its later years, it became a flophouse. People without much money could rent rooms there for cheap. "No telling who died there," Chuck told me.

The people who experience most of the haunting are the ones who work in the main office where all the security monitors are located. When they're sitting at a desk working on paperwork, they frequently catch something out of their peripheral vision. It feels as though someone has walked up to the long bay of windows in front of them and is staring at them through the window. When they look up, no one is there.

Chuck introduced me to a man named Rick who was working in the office. Rick has experienced his fair share of paranormal happenings. Not only has he witnessed the shapes in front of the window, but he's also seen an actual ghost.

"I walked downstairs to the chlorine room one night. I turned and there was a woman standing there in a white Victorian dress. She was only there for a few seconds before she disappeared, but I saw her clear as day," Rick said. The experience startled him but didn't frighten him, which seems to be common among the Water Works Department employees.

"I see a lot of stuff on the cameras too," Rick added. He said that the month of October is the most active.

Chuck has also witnessed the occurrences. He's been employed at the Water Works Department since 2000 and has been in charge since 2005. He started out as a meter reader and then became a third-shift operator. That was when he first started experiencing strange things.

As he worked in front of the windows, he swore he saw someone walk up to the window. When he looked up, nobody was there. "I thought people were messing with me at the time. It was like people were ducking down in front of the window," he said. He began talking to others and quickly learned that it happened all the time.

Chuck began wondering if the activity was due to electromagnetic energy created by all the equipment, so he invited a local ghost hunting group to investigate the property. In preparation for their arrival, Chuck turned off all the machines so they wouldn't interfere with any of the paranormal equipment. But it didn't matter. Soon after the group showed up, all of their freshly charged batteries immediately died. We've also had this same phenomenon happen to us during investigations. Ghosts need energy to manifest. They will pull energy from easily accessible sources, and batteries seem to be one of their favorites. If your batteries die instantly, it's a fairly good indicator that the property is haunted.

The ghost hunting group spent several hours investigating the building and found it to be one of the most haunted locations they'd ever witnessed. During the investigation, one of the women was recording an EVP (electronic voice phenomenon) session. They sat quietly and asked questions, hoping for a ghostly response to be captured on the digital recorders. Upon playback, they clearly heard a woman say, "Hey, Chuck!"

A 1913 photo of the Water Works Department. *Courtesy of the Posey County Historical Society.*

While the response was stunning, it wasn't necessarily surprising. After all the experiences he's had there, Chuck expected almost anything.

As he stood there talking to me, more stories came to him. He told me about an experience he had there years ago, before they replaced the original water filters. As he walked into the room, he saw the shadow of a man on the side of one of the concrete tanks. It was so precise, he fully expected to walk around the tank and find a person standing there, but the room was empty. It just became another story in a long list of strange encounters.

Before I left, Chuck introduced me to a man named Tim Ghrist.

Like everyone else I talked to that day, Tim wanted to assure me that he wasn't crazy. He didn't believe in ghosts before he started working there. When some of his coworkers shared their stories with him, he mentally rolled his eyes. It didn't take long before he became a believer.

The first time it happened, he couldn't believe what he was seeing. As he sat at the desk, someone clearly came up to the window in front of him. When he looked up, no one was there. Figuring the guys were playing a prank on him, he walked out the door and took a look, shocked to see that no one was there.

"I work in here by myself a lot. There's definitely been a presence. It's nothing fearful. They just want to know what I'm doing," Tim told me.

Occasionally, he'll see orbs on the camera in the chorine room. "It comes toward the camera like it's going to pop right through the screen. It's fascinating and ominous at the same time," Tim told me, rubbing his arms as if to wipe away the goosebumps the memory created.

"We've approached this skeptically, but there's no denying we've seen what we've seen. It's not like car lights are making shadows because there aren't any windows. We see distinctive human shapes," Chuck added.

While I stood there trying to absorb all the information Chuck had already given me, he gave me something else to think about.

"Do you know about the sinking of the *Cotton Blossom* and the *Jewel*?" he asked. I had a vague recollection of the story after hearing it from Ray Kessler, but he filled me in on the details.

In 1918, the Mount Vernon area was hit with an especially cold spell. It was so frigid that the river began to freeze. A lavish steamboat called the *Cotton Blossom* and the steamer that towed it, *Jewel*, were tied up at the riverfront when the deep freeze occurred.

It happened so quickly that Captain Otto Hitner, who was in charge of the boat, didn't have time to react before they were frozen in. The moving ice pushed both boats farther down the river in front of the Water Works

A photo taken during the 1937 flood. If you look in the foreground, you can see the McFaddin family monument stone partially submerged under the water. *Courtesy of the Posey County Historical Society.*

The *Cotton Blossom. Courtesy of the Posey County Historical Society.*

Department, where they both eventually sank. Chuck said if you look on Google Earth, you can see the shadows of the vessels. They are submerged forty feet beneath the water and are protected by the U.S. Army Corps of Engineers.

Back in 2015, when the Water Works Department added its new intakes, there was a labor dispute, and the first group of divers quit. When the second divers showed up, Chuck laughingly told them it was due to a monster catfish. He said the first group accidentally knocked a wall off the side of the *Cotton Blossom* and a giant catfish came out. The intakes have air scours on them, so when one switches over to the other, it makes a huge air bubble out in the river that's nearly twenty feet across. He told them that was the catfish.

Thankfully, they didn't believe him, but Chuck says it is a surprise for boaters on the river when they see the air bubble. "We don't do it if we see boaters out there, but sometimes they show up and see it," he said with a laugh.

The haunting at the Water Works Department is legendary. In a land so permeated with history, it's no wonder that a few souls decided to linger. Judging by the stories, they're enjoying their afterlife.

Keck Motor Building Haunting

Formerly located at 115 West Fifth Street
Mount Vernon, Indiana

Sometimes, ghosts aren't supernatural entities; they are nothing more than memories of the past. We call this residual energy. It happens when the land itself records a memory and replays it for those who care to listen.

The city of Mount Vernon is filled with residual energy. You can sense it drifting in the wind. It's so palpable; it's almost tangible. The sensation is especially strong on Main Street.

From its humble beginnings as a river town, Mount Vernon eventually grew to its current population of 6,500. Its dynamics evolved to become a factory town, employing thousands of people in the local area. The river, while still boasting a busy port, became an equal mixture of recreation and industry.

Many of the old buildings from the town's early beginnings have been torn down and replaced with new structures, but several turn-of-the-century buildings still remain. What you won't see are the layers of history on each lot. A good example is the Alexandrian Public Library.

In 1885, a woman named Matilda Greathouse Alexander decided that the town needed a library. She took over a small section of the old courthouse and filled it with one hundred books. As the popularity of the library grew, the town decided that a larger building was needed. Soon, a massive brick

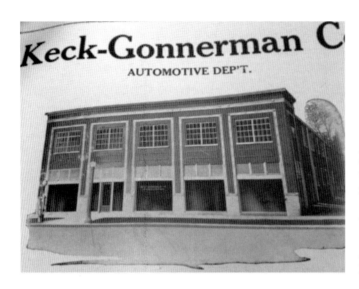

Left: The Keck Gonnerman business was open from 1873 to the 1950s. *Courtesy of Richard Keck.*

Opposite: The old Alexandrian Public Library.

building was constructed, boasting tall columns and a stately set of stairs that led to a set of grand double doors. Walking in was always an ethereal experience, taking your breath away.

As a child, it was my first experience with libraries. As an intuitive, introverted child, I was instantly enamored. Having already devoured all the books at home, I was elated to discover an entire building filled to the brim with additional reading material.

Back in the 1970s, children had a much longer leash than they do today. I would climb onto my bicycle during the summer months and explore the town, not returning home until I was either hungry or it was growing dark. One of my favorite haunts was the library.

I can remember walking into the cool depths of the building, feeling the somber, yet monumental, sensations that only an old building can evoke. It felt substantial and significant, a sacred space for those of us who worshiped books. I also felt the presence of a ghost.

She was old and motherly, the kind of woman who would take you by the hand and help you find the perfect book. In some ways, I feel like she guided me to the books that would mold me into the adult I eventually became. I was always drawn to the mysteries, to Nancy Drew, Trixie Belden and the Bobbsey Twins, which eventually transformed to Agatha Christie, Shirley Jackson and Stephen King.

By 1985, the library had outgrown the old building. A new building was built across the street, and the old library building became the police station before becoming town offices and then finally being retired. It

now sits empty, looking as grand and dignified as it did when it was first constructed.

I've always wondered what happens to the ghosts when their building is gone or their business is moved. Do they stay with the land, or do they move to the new location? If a new building is built on the same land, do the ghosts simply begin haunting the new building?

While no one at the new library is aware of a haunting, it doesn't mean the ghosts aren't there. Sometimes it just takes the right person or a unique situation to draw them out of hiding. Considering the circumstances, I wouldn't be surprised if a haunting doesn't present itself at some point in the library's future. The reason has more to do with the land the new library currently sits on.

Back in 1917, a different building occupied that property. The large brick building housed the Keck Gonnerman factory. It manufactured farm tractors and threshing machines, which were all the rage with farmers. The machines shook and beat the crops to separate the seeds and kernels, saving the farmers a great deal of time in the fields.

The Keck Gonnerman business lasted until the 1940s, when the factory closed its doors forever. The Keck family took over the building and filled the space with their automobile dealership and garage, which had previously been located in a different building.

Richard Keck grew up in the family business. He recalled, "Keck Gonnerman was in business from 1873 until the 1950s. They started the auto department in 1907. My grandfather Grover was tapped to run it. It was originally a Cadillac dealer, but in 1912, they switched to Ford. In 1917, they built this new building on the corner of Sixth and Main. In the 1920s, they bought Gonnerman out of the auto division.

"I worked there on and off when I was younger, before joining my dad, Bill Keck, in 1980. As a kid, the building was very spooky," he said.

He remembers feeling a chill down his spine any time he had to walk into the service area at night, and he wasn't the only one. Everyone who worked there experienced the activity.

"If you ever went into the service area at night when it was dark, you turned on every light as quickly as possible. You would hear strange noises, clanking on pipes and just odd things. There were stories from men working on their own cars late at night. They would be under the car looking up, and something would be looking down on them through the engine compartment," he said.

Originally, the service department was upstairs, but it was moved downstairs in the 1950s. A body shop was created upstairs, which apparently confused the ghost in the building. Ghosts often view their surroundings as they were back when they were alive. Even though it looks vastly different to the living, the dead sometimes still see it as it used to be. This can explain why people frequently see ghosts walk through walls. If they dug through the history of the property, they would probably discover there used to be a door where the ghost walks through.

Over time, people began experiencing paranormal activity on a regular basis. They would hear strange banging sounds when they walked around the empty building. It seemed especially loud if they were there alone at night. While some dismissed it as imagination, others were quite spooked by the antics of the shop ghost.

"Once a guy quit on the spot because he came in early to clean the place, and something up there scared him," Richard told me.

The eighteen-year-old employee was hired to clean the body shop but only spent a few minutes upstairs before he came down yelling, "I quit! I quit!" He wouldn't talk about it and simply told them he was never coming back before running out the door.

It didn't take long before the ghost was identified.

One day, a man brought in an old photograph that was taken in 1928. The men gathered around and marveled at the old-fashioned clothing and the way the shop looked back in its heyday, but one man was visibly shaken.

"What's the matter, Lou?" someone asked him.

This 1928 photo was taken when the new Model A Ford came out, replacing the Model T. Alpf White is in gray overalls. Oscar is the guy in front on the other side of the car wearing a bow tie. *Courtesy of Richard Keck.*

Ignoring the question, he leaned forward and pointed at one of the men in the photo.

"Who is that man?" Lou asked.

Oscar Bottomley, who was also in the picture as a younger man said, "Why, that's Alpf White! Why do you ask?"

"Because that's the man I've been seeing in the body shop," Lou told them. "He was the one looking down at me when I was working on a car."

It makes sense that Alpf White would continue to hang around the dealership. He had a strong connection to the business. Alpf was the service manager in the 1940s. He was a dedicated company man who spent many years at the dealership. When Richard's dad and his uncle John took over, Alpf was demoted to make room for the Keck sons. He had a heart attack soon after.

While he was at the hospital, he frequently asked his visitors how the dealership was doing. He died shortly afterward and apparently returned to the building instead of enjoying his ever after in heaven. People say he died of a broken heart.

Was Alpf still haunting the building? It makes total sense. It was the one place that was the most important to him. He didn't want to leave and not know what was going on.

"It sounds silly, but there was something spooky about that building for decades, and lots of people claimed it," Richard said.

One night, they were having a Christmas party at the old showroom. As the guests sat around, they began noticing that a pipe kept clanking every time someone mentioned Alpf's name.

Bennie Watson was a salesman at Keck Motor Company for thirty years. When he first started, Richard was only twelve years old. He also experienced the haunting. "I've been in there at night, and you can hear somebody upstairs, but there was never anybody there," he told me.

I don't know if Alpf White is still lingering on the property or if he moved on when the building burned down in 1982. I've been inside the new Alexandrian Public Library and have felt the presence of at least one ghost, but it hangs back in the corner, not willing to communicate.

Hopefully, Alpf finally crossed over to heaven. Only time will tell.

POSEY COUNTY
SHERIFF'S DEPARTMENT

1201 O'Donnell Road
Mount Vernon, Indiana

Why would a ghost haunt the sheriff's department? It certainly isn't an ideal place to spend an afterlife. If given a choice, I'd pick somewhere warm and tropical, like Tahiti or Hawaii.

I was curious about it and began digging into the history, wondering if there was more to the story. As it turns out, there was. The haunting had more to do with the land than it did with the building.

Back in the mid-1800s, the poor and the infirm were cared for in several homes in Posey County. While this system worked for a while, it soon became too much to handle. In 1857, a central facility was built near the town of Poseyville. By 1870, there were twenty inmates, as they called them, ranging in age from one to ninety years old. By 1889, they had outgrown that facility as well.

Thirty acres of land were soon purchased on the outskirts of Mount Vernon, and ground was broken on a brand-new asylum. The massive two-story brick building was laid out in a cross design, with women being housed on one wing of the cross and men on the other. The center arm of the cross was used for patients deemed to be insane.

The new county infirmary opened its doors in 1890 and received twenty-two inmates from the old Poseyville asylum. Many of them had been there for nearly thirty years. Saying goodbye to their old superintendent and

A current photo of the Posey County Sheriff's Department.

caretakers was a tearful moment as they found themselves surrounded by brand-new staff. It must have been terrifying for them to be shuffled from one place to another and to be put under the care of strangers. They loved their old caretakers like family, but they didn't have any choice in the matter. They went where they were sent.

For the era, it was a decent facility, costing nearly $26,000. By June 1890, the gas lights had been replaced with electric lighting, which was exciting for the new residents. By 1910, Superintendent George W. Alldredge, matron Nancy Curtis and cook Jessie Davis were caring for twenty-seven inmates.

Inmates were admitted to the poor farm for a variety of reasons. Some were simply too poor to provide for themselves, while others were there for conditions like epilepsy, feeble-mindedness and insanity.

The county infirmary had a working farm on the property with chickens and hogs. Inmates who were physically capable were expected to help with farm work. They took care of the livestock and tended to the multiple gardens. Most enjoyed the work because it gave them a sense of purpose.

When inmates died, they didn't have far to go. A cemetery was located behind the building. Records were kept of the burials, but you'd have a difficult time locating the actual graves today. It's possible some, if not all, of the graves were moved to another cemetery in the area. It's also highly probable that many of the bodies still remain in unmarked graves.

It wasn't all doom and gloom though. A June 1932 newspaper article tells the story of romance. Two inmates, Clara Dipple and Charles Hust, both fifty-two years old, left the infirmary in true Romeo and Juliet fashion by climbing out a window. While their story is endearing, it wasn't meant to last. Clara returned weeks later, reporting that Charles was mean to her and wouldn't marry her, so she returned to her home at the infirmary.

My friend Rosie Benton remembers visiting her grandmother there. "The patients were very well cared for," she told me.

She remembers one woman who lived there who was always dressed to the nines. "She had bright rouge on her cheeks and was always decked out every time I visited. Nothing was ever out of place," she said.

Rosie said that while the majority of the building had a cheery atmosphere, there was an area that always gave her a chill. It was at an intersection where you could go upstairs to the men's section or to the area where the administrators stayed. "When you went to that intersection, you could feel something there."

Her grandmother said it also gave her the heebie-jeebies. "Grandma told me she often saw misty shapes floating around there," Rosie said.

By early 1972, the building was in poor shape, and the inmates, now referred to as patients, were moved to a facility in Evansville. The county infirmary closed its doors forever.

By 1975, the building was razed, and the property was soon utilized for another purpose. The sheriff's department needed a larger building. Soon, it was built on the same site as the old poor farm.

Cue the ghosts.

It wasn't long before staff in the new building began experiencing strange things. Many of them dismissed it as their imagination, but the sightings were so frequent that it became harder and harder for the disbelievers to maintain their skepticism.

Years ago, the Posey County dispatch was in the same building as the sheriff's department. During the day, the building felt normal, but as soon as darkness fell, everything changed. The dispatchers began seeing things. They would be sitting at their stations when they'd catch movement out of the corners of their eyes. They'd turn and see a white mist roll across the floor. It always came out of nowhere and disappeared just as quickly as it appeared.

When it first began happening, they were alarmed, as anyone would be. They tried to find a source for the mist, initially thinking it was smoke or something coming from the electrical or heating system, but nothing was amiss.

The mist itself would have been bad enough, but they soon began seeing something even more frightening.

I talked to a man I'll call Jake. He wishes to remain anonymous. Jake was a paramedic for thirty-six years and was stationed at the sheriff's department. One night, he came back from an ambulance run at around two o'clock in the morning. He admits he was tired, but what he saw was more than a fatigue-induced hallucination.

"I was heading to the control room to get my times for the run. As I was walking down the hallway, I happened to glance to my left. There was a little kitchen off to the side with an ice machine that everyone used for their drinks. There was a man standing there, staring at me," he said.

Jake stopped mid-step and just stared, because what he saw went well beyond normal. "He was wearing a gray rain slicker and had on one of those Cape Cod rain hats, you know, the kind you see on the fish stick boxes," he told me.

He glanced away, and when he looked back, the figure was gone.

He tried to dismiss it. "I was tired and thought the shadows might have been playing tricks on me," he said, but he had to reconsider this after he learned that others had also seen the man in the rain slicker.

Several months later, he was sitting in the break room. Several people were also there, including one of the deputies.

"Has anyone seen the ghost lately?" the deputy asked.

Jake was stunned. "Ghost?" he asked.

One of the dispatchers laughed. "Let me guess, the man in the rain slicker?"

As Jake sat listening, the deputy and the dispatcher began talking about the ghost. Supposedly, the man lived on the property when it was a poor farm. One night during a storm, he went outside in his rain slicker and hanged himself, and he has been haunting the land ever since.

Jake's next encounter was enough to leave him stunned. The EMTs had quarters in the basement of the building. It gave them a place to nap between shifts. It was located directly below the booking room. Jake said it was common to hear a commotion overhead from time to time. "You could sometimes hear the sally doors bang open, especially if there was a drunk in there," he said.

He was in bed, facing the wall, when he was awakened by the sound of a door slamming overhead. He glanced at his watch. It was one o'clock in the morning.

He had a hard time getting back to sleep, so he rolled over. There was a couch on the other side of the room, and the ghost in the rain slicker was sitting on it, staring at him.

"He was there for a good ten seconds before I blinked and he disappeared," Jake said.

Surprisingly, Jake wasn't frightened by the apparition.

"I didn't feel threatened. It was just like, 'well, there you are.'"

Another person also experienced the ghost in the same area. A female deputy was taking a nap in the basement when she woke up and realized someone was giving her a back rub. She jolted awake and turned to discover that the room was empty. No one was there.

The sightings were so frequent that nearly everyone who worked there saw the ghost at one point or another. One time, the encounter left a deputy bloodied.

The deputy often walked along behind the cells to listen in on the inmates. He would even remove his shoes so they couldn't hear him. One night, as he was making his rounds, something unexpected happened to him. He felt something zoom past him. The encounter startled him so badly that he took off running and ran into a wall, bloodying his own nose. He turned on the lights to see what had rushed past him, but the hallway was empty.

Laura Frisby also experienced some unusual incidents. When she started working there in 1994, she was nonplussed by the ghostly lore. She wasn't necessarily a skeptic, but the stories were too outlandish to take at face value. "I'd have to see it to believe it," she said.

When something odd finally happened, it wasn't what she expected. Instead of seeing the same man in a raincoat that everyone else saw, she experienced something even more phenomenal.

She was working a midnight shift in the dispatcher's area. The area was U-shaped with a tall counter. From her position, if someone walked past, she could only see them from the shoulders up. As she was sitting there, she caught movement out of the corner of her eye and turned to look, surprised to see a woman on the other side of the counter. The woman had long, straight hair that was parted in the middle. Instead of flowing to her shoulders, her hair molded closely to her head. At first, Laura thought it was another dispatcher named Brenda, who also had long, thin hair. She started to say something to her when something else caught her attention.

There was a round mirror in the hallway to allow the dispatchers to see if someone was approaching. When she glanced at it, no one was reflected in the mirror. If it was Brenda, Laura should have seen her reflection.

The woman continued down the hallway. Laura sat there in stunned silence, not sure what she'd just witnessed. Could it be a ghost? It didn't look like a ghost. It looked like a regular person. "It wasn't foggy or misty, like what you think a ghost should look like, so I wasn't sure," she said.

She eased out of her chair and walked to the hallway, following the path the woman had just taken.

"I thought that she might have ducked down below the counter, but when I got there, no one was there. There was nowhere for the woman to have gone. She just vanished," she said.

Considering where she was, she couldn't just let it go, so she called one of the jailers. When he arrived, he looked at her expectantly, waiting for her to fill him in on why she'd called him.

"At first, I didn't want to tell him what I saw. I didn't want him to think I was crazy, but I finally just told him," she said. The jailer looked around but didn't see anyone, so she was left wondering what she had witnessed.

The next day, she shared her story with another dispatcher and learned some startling information. There had been a head-on crash the previous night. All the occupants had burned to death inside the car. Instead of removing the bodies at the scene, they towed the entire car to the sheriff's department to extract them, preventing onlookers from seeing the shocking sight.

"One of those girls who died in that car had long, straight hair, just like you described," the dispatcher told her, giving her a head-to-toe chill.

The woman was young and pregnant; her life came to an end well before it was supposed to. Was she wandering around the building, trying to figure out what had happened to her? No one will ever know for certain, but the probability is high. Traumatic deaths often result in a haunting.

"You can write me off as crazy. I don't care. I know what I saw," Laura said.

Dispatch was moved to another area in 1997, and Laura didn't have any more experiences, but she did recall something that happened to someone else there. "There was a trustee who had an encounter," she told me, and then filled me in on the rest of the story.

The jail had trustees. These were inmates who were incarcerated on misdemeanor charges. They were people who could be trusted and had earned more privileges for good behavior. One of the trustees went into the kitchen to make a pot of coffee. As he was scooping the grounds into the coffeepot, a man in a dark raincoat and hat walked in and just stared at him. The trustee asked the man if he wanted some coffee, but when he turned around, the man was gone.

Perplexed, the trustee went up to one of the women who was working in the kitchen and asked where the man went, but she had no idea what he was talking about.

"What man?" she asked.

"Some guy came in, and I asked him if he wanted a cup of coffee. When I turned around, he was gone," he said.

The woman laughed. "Was he wearing a raincoat and hat?" she asked, watching as his face turned pale.

"How did you know that?" he asked.

"You must have seen the ghost," she told him.

From that moment forward, the trustee refused to go into the kitchen alone.

Erin Wolfe also shared stories with me. She was a corrections officer from 2003 until 2018. Like many others, when she started working there, she heard the ghostly lore but didn't think much about it until she had her own confrontations.

Erin never liked the basement. She couldn't put her finger on what made it so eerie, but she didn't like being down there. When the sheriff asked her to go down there to look for something, she followed directions, even though it gave her the creeps. When she got to the bottom of the stairs, the feeling of being watched came over her strongly. She looked around, fully expecting to find someone standing there, but the room was empty.

Gathering her courage, she made her way to the middle of the room. Without warning, she heard something that made her blood go cold. It was the sound of a little girl laughing. It wasn't just laughter though; it was the kind you heard in a horror movie. She stood there, frozen to the spot, the sound going right through her. Finally, she bolted up the stairs, telling the sheriff she couldn't find what he was looking for. After that, she never went down into the basement alone again.

At the time, she wondered if it had something to do with the old display case that was stored in the basement. It contained some gruesome relics from Mount Vernon's past, including two nooses from the last hanging, as well as shackles used on prisoners. It wasn't until she learned about the history of the land that she began to understand why she might have heard the child's mischievous giggle.

She searched through the death records from the county infirmary and was saddened to see children's names on the list. She felt herself go still inside as she read through the list. Several of the children were little girls.

"It could have been one of them," she whispered to herself. Being a mother, she couldn't imagine the heartache of a child being separated from her family. Why would she stay in the cold, dark basement?

As much as she wanted to, she couldn't avoid the basement. She had to go down there frequently. It was part of her job. It was where all the inmates' records were kept. True to her promise, though, she never again went down there alone.

One time, she was down there with one of the men she worked with. Everyone knew how uneasy she was in the basement, and she always worried they were going to prank her. She kept a close eye on them, just in case.

As they walked past a row of old office wall dividers, the man gasped and then bolted for the stairs. He nearly knocked Erin over in his panic to retreat from the basement. Erin wasn't sure what had frightened him, but she wasn't hanging around to find out.

When they got upstairs, she asked him what had happened. The man was as white as a sheet. "Something growled at me," he said, visibly shaken. It took him a minute to get the full story out, but when he finally did, it was enough to leave them all unnerved.

As he walked past the rows of old office dividers, he heard a deep guttural growl. It wasn't the kind of growl you'd expect to hear in the basement of the sheriff's department. It was something you'd hear in your nightmares.

Weeks later, Erin learned that the jail matron also had an odd experience that corresponded with what had happened to her. The matron's role was to monitor and care for the female inmates of the jail. Their matron at the time was a woman named Sheila. She normally came in early to take care of the commissary. She was in her office doing paperwork when she heard the unmistakable sound of a little girl laughing, followed by the sound of running.

Thinking it was another coworker who was there with her daughter, Sheila pushed her candy bowl to the edge of her desk, ready to greet the youngster. After a minute or two, she didn't hear any other sounds, so she got up from her desk and looked out the window. The parking lot was empty. No one else was there. Was it the same child Erin heard?

Sometime later, the commissary was moved to the basement. The matron went down there and realized it was padlocked. She came upstairs and asked someone to go down with her. As they approached the locked door, the padlock lifted up, completely defying gravity, and began to twist in midair. They just stood there and watched it, not believing what they were seeing.

With everything that had happened to her, Erin still hadn't had her creepiest encounter. It happened one night as she was sitting in the control room with two coworkers, Brian and Beth. The three of them were working the midnight shift.

All of a sudden, Brian stopped talking and began staring at one of the monitors.

"What's the matter?" Erin asked him.

"Oh, nothing. I just thought I saw something on the recreation yard monitor," he said.

Erin and Beth moved closer to the monitor, and then they saw it too. A black shape walked across the yard.

As they stared, gape-mouthed, the shape began to take the form of a man. It was darker than a normal shadow, as though it had been cut from the fabric of reality. It walked across the yard and then disappeared.

The three were dumbstruck. The recreation yard, often referred to as the "rec yard," had walls on all four sides and was completely enclosed with barbed wire along the top. There was no way anyone could have wandered in there.

The paranormal encounters were endless. On another occasion, Erin was sitting in the control room when a pair of rubber shower shoes went flying across the room. She didn't see them move but knew where they had been and heard the thud as they landed on the ground nearly fifteen feet away. After that, she didn't want to be in the control room by herself.

If that wasn't bad enough, weird things also began happening at her home. She never had anything odd happen until she came home one day and discovered all her shampoo and conditioner bottles in the tub.

She thought it was strange because it had never happened before, but she didn't give it much thought. She put them back where they belonged and forgot about it until it happened again.

It made no sense. As hard as she tried, she couldn't come up with a rational explanation for it. As the weeks went past, it happened almost on a daily basis.

Adding to the strangeness, she began having other bizarre incidents. As she got out of the shower one day, she discovered that the door to her medicine cabinet was wide open. She couldn't remember opening it but brushed it off. When a lightbulb burst overhead, sending a shower of glass down on top of her, she began to wonder if her bathroom was haunted.

"What were the odds of that?" she wondered. "And why the bathroom?" Nothing made sense about it, but it was beginning to truly creep her out.

Others in her household also began experiencing the haunting. She often worked midnight shifts. As she left for the night, one of her sons decided to sleep in her bedroom while she was gone. When she came home the next morning, she found him in his own bed.

"I thought you were going to sleep in my room," she said to him.

He gave her an odd look. "I was going to, but I woke up and saw a mannequin in your bathroom, so I went to my room."

The thought unnerved her. Had she brought something home from the jail?

A friend recommended putting crosses and crucifixes around the room to help drive the ghosts away. She didn't waste any time. She went out and purchased as many crosses as she could find and hung them all around the bathroom. Thankfully, that seemed to take care of things.

Years later, she learned she wasn't the only one who experienced the medicine cabinet opening on its own. Her son told her he'd had the very same thing happen, and he knew the cabinet was closed when he got into the shower.

The sheriff's department was eventually updated. A new addition was built, and the inmates were moved to the new section. The old jail area is now home to offices. The changes seem to have appeased the ghosts because no further activity has been reported.

I have a feeling there's more to this story that we'll never know. Ghosts don't usually simply vanish. I'd like to believe that someone went in and did a cleansing, releasing them from their earthly ties. It's one of those things I might never learn the answer to.

I just hope they finally found some peace.

FUNK'S CARPET SHOWROOM

220 West Fourth Street
Mount Vernon, Indiana

When Traci Hoehn moved into an apartment above Funk's Carpet Showroom, she had no idea it was haunted. It wasn't long, though, before she realized she shared the space with an invisible roommate. The ghost seemed to gravitate toward her apartment, seldom migrating to other areas of the building. She would feel the wayward spirit from time to time, but the encounters were never scary. Over time, other ghosts have come in and out, drifting in like transients looking for a place to settle.

Traci is a friend of mine and helps me with my paranormal investigations and ghost walks. Due to our hobbies, we sometimes end up with hitchhikers. These invisible beings latch onto us and follow us to our homes. Such was the case with the Aqua Velva Man.

Shortly after we did a paranormal investigation together, Traci immediately began smelling the iconic men's cologne in her home. It was so strong it was as though a man stood at the foot of her bed after dowsing himself with the powerful liquid. She would smell it off and on during the day. In the beginning, she looked for a source of the smell and soon came to realize she wouldn't find one. It became a curious topic of conversation. Why would someone identify himself in the afterlife as a person who doused himself in cologne? We've smelled cigarette and pipe smoke occasionally when encountering the dead. On occasion, we've smelled women's perfume but never something as identifying as Aqua Velva cologne.

Funk's Carpet Showroom today.

As someone who is experienced in dealing with the souls of the dead, Traci simply ignored him. It took several weeks, but eventually he moved on to somewhere else. "He finally got bored of me," she said.

Traci also has one female ghost that she calls her "house ghost." "She strikes me as being very proper. I think she is somehow associated with the time when a beauty salon utilized the space. We get along well, as we both have respect for each other's boundaries," Traci said.

The house ghost makes herself known by moving objects in the middle of the night. It almost sounds as though someone is rustling around the apartment, poking through her belongings. When Traci gets up to investigate, she can never figure out which item was moved.

The house ghost has another horrifying habit. "She has also been known to sit on the foot of my bed while I am trying to fall asleep. Usually, I just tell her that I am too tired to talk, and she leaves," Traci said. On a recent occasion, the ghost actually tried to climb into bed with her. She felt the mattress depress, but before she was able to tell the ghost to leave her alone, it crawled up to the top of the bed behind her. Traci leapt from her bed and was horrified at what she saw. The shape of a body was imprinted on the covers in the space directly behind where she'd been sleeping.

"All right. That's enough!" she told the ghost. Seconds later, she watched as her blankets flattened back out again.

Another woman, whom I'll call Sarah, had a similar experience. She moved into the same apartment years before Traci rented it. At first, she didn't notice anything odd. On occasion, she felt as though someone was watching her, but she brushed it off as nerves. She was there for several weeks before she had the fright of her life.

In the middle of the night, she felt the distinct sensation of someone sitting on the end of her bed. She felt the bed sink with the weight and heard the springs squeak. She jumped out of bed and turned on the light, horrified that someone might have broken into her apartment. What she saw was equally terrifying. The room was empty.

The woman moved out the next morning.

Traci has nerves of steel, something I've witnessed time and time again. We once spent an entire night investigating nearby Waverly Hills Sanatorium in Louisville, Kentucky. Waverly Hills is a huge building that once housed tuberculosis patients and is a known paranormal hotspot. Traci was always the first one to venture into the darkest, creepiest rooms, forcing the rest of us to up our games. When we do public ghost hunts, I always put Traci in the basement of whatever building we're investigating, because she's often the only one who can handle it.

When Traci's former sister-in-law, Jyl, moved into the apartment next door with her two children, she also began experiencing strange phenomena. Unlike Traci, Jyl found the activity frightening. If she had something odd happen, she would ask Traci to do a cleansing of her apartment. Traci also had a word with the house ghost, asking her to refrain from entering Jyl's apartment.

"I told her she was welcome in my apartment because, after all, she was here first," Traci said.

That tactic seemed to work, and their apartment remained relatively quiet. There were occasional incidences that required addressing. One of the most unexplainable events occurred as Jyl's daughter Lexi was trying to fall asleep one night.

As she lay in her bed, she noticed a ball of white light on the ceiling. Slowly, it descended from the ceiling to the floor, nearly lighting up the entire room with its brilliance. It was enough to send Lexi fleeing from her bedroom.

Several other times, as Jyl left for work in the mornings, she saw Traci's front door close. For months, she thought she was being too noisy, causing Traci to peek out the door, but she later learned this wasn't the case. Traci had been sound asleep in her bed every time.

The house ghost seemed to be agreeable with the arrangement, but she often became agitated when she felt her space was being compromised.

"There is a hallway behind the apartments that we use for storage. Jyl primarily used it to keep the kids' Christmas presents out of view. During the month leading up to Christmas, more and more noises could be heard from the hallway, along with the sounds of pacing steps. Jyl absolutely hated going in the back hall and always felt like she was being watched there," Traci said.

While we know that old buildings often hold on to spiritual energy, a primary reason for the haunting could be due to one of its early purposes. The Weisinger's Funeral Home was once located where Funk's Carpet now resides. It was established in 1866 by Henry Weisinger. The main floor was used for offices and funeral services, but the upstairs was once the heart of the funeral home.

In the space where Traci and Jyl's apartments now occupy were four showrooms and an embalming room. The business was taken over by A.V. Weisinger and his son, Merle, in 1904. Since that time, the funeral home closed and other various businesses took its spot, including a beauty shop.

Funk's Carpet Showroom opened in 1986 and was in operation until it closed its doors in January 2022. The current owners are now looking for new tenants for the first floor. Let's just hope they also have nerves of steel. They might need them.

ROBIN HILL

917 Mill Street
Mount Vernon, Indiana

Whenn I first announced that I would be writing a book about the hauntings in Posey County, most people asked me if I planned to write about Robin Hill. Historically, it was a relevant part of Mount Vernon, and the haunting was supposed to be phenomenal; but no one would tell me about their experiences.

All I had to go on were the local legends and the fact that the SyFy Channel's show *Ghost Hunters* investigated there years ago. *Ghost Hunters* didn't find anything, but that didn't stop the rumors.

I was ready to give up on including Robin Hill in this book until, like magic, the stories started rolling in.

The first story came from a woman I'll call Diana, who wishes to remain anonymous. She grew up in Mount Vernon and lived fairly close to Robin Hill. At the tender age of seven, she probably didn't know the history of the property, but she did know it was creepy.

It was an old house, built in 1836. It was originally called the Lowry House, named after its first owner, William Lowry. At some point, he decided to change the name to Robin Hill. Some say it's due to the abnormal abundance of robins that flock to the lawn every spring.

During its history, it changed hands several times. At one point, it was called Popcorn Hill until a man named George F. Zimmerman purchased it and changed it back to Robin Hill.

A current-day photo of Robin Hill.

Diana probably didn't know the history, but she'd probably heard the rumors about it being an Underground Railroad house. According to legend, there was a hidden room in the basement that connected to a tunnel that led to the river. Escaped slaves from the South could use the house as a resting place before they made their way farther north to freedom. While Indiana was a border state, there's no proof there were any Underground Railroad stations in Posey County. People who have owned Robin Hill have fervently disputed the rumor.

The stories probably started because there used to be a creek near the property that led to the river. It became so overgrown that the toppled-over weeds resembled a tunnel when viewed from the river. Regardless of Diana's knowledge about the house, it made a very good shortcut. Her mother's friend lived next door. She and her sister would often cut through the backyard to get to their mother's friend's house.

All the kids were terrified of the house. Some of the older kids tried to break in from time to time to look for the ghosts, but it was difficult because the windows were boarded up. It looked exactly like what you'd expect from a haunted house. The plantation-style house was two stories tall with substantial white columns flanking the front door. In its day, it was a grande dame, but it had lost all its charm in the passing years.

One day, Diana was cutting through the yard alone when something caught her eye. She turned mid-step to see an older woman with gray hair standing in the doorway. Diana thought it was odd because she was certain the door had been boarded up the last time she walked past. Dusk was beginning to settle on the horizon, but it was still light enough to get a good look at the woman.

Fearful she was going to get into trouble for being in the yard, Diana started to run away, but the woman waved to her. "Come inside for a snack, sweetie," she called, beckoning Diana with her hand.

Diana hesitated. The woman looked friendly, but something about her didn't seem right. Following her gut instincts, Diana darted across the lawn to get to her mother's friend's house. When she got there, she told them about what she'd experienced.

"But honey, nobody lives there. The house is all boarded up," her mother told her.

"But I talked to her. She asked me to come in for a snack," Diana protested, but neither woman would believe her. They told her to stop making up stories.

Later, as she and her mother were walking back home on the street, Diana looked toward the house and was stunned by what she saw. The doorway the woman had been leaning out of was boarded up like all the other windows and doors on the house.

After that experience, Diana made it a point to race past the house, and she never cut through the backyard again.

Another woman who grew up in Mount Vernon had a similar experience. When she would walk past, she sometimes saw a woman in a long white dress standing on the balcony. If she blinked, the woman disappeared. Other times when she walked past, craning her neck to look for the woman on the balcony, she'd hear a loud bang inside the house. It was enough to send her running.

Many others have reported seeing shadowy figures in the windows. Sometimes people would hear the toilets flush when no one was at home.

Tony Viviano grew up in Mount Vernon during the 1980s and was well aware of the haunting of Robin Hill. During that period, the mansion was abandoned and boarded up.

"We all heard the ghost stories," he told me. "But the best one happened to a friend of mine's stepfather. I was there when he told us about it."

The friend's stepfather was an officer on the Mount Vernon Police Department. One night, he got a call about a possible break-in there. Needing to check it out, he walked around the inside of the house with a flashlight, thinking that kids had broken in to do some ghost hunting. The rumors about the haunting were legendary, and teenagers often dared one another to go inside. As he walked room to room, shining his light around, he fully expected to find a group of kids hiding in a corner. But that's not what he found.

As he got to one of the bedrooms, he had the fright of his life. There was a life-sized ragdoll sitting in a rocking chair. The sight of it startled him because he wasn't expecting to see a human-shaped form in the house. He turned away, laughing at himself for getting spooked so easily, but when he turned back, the doll was gone. He panned around with his flashlight and discovered the doll was now sitting on the bed. That was enough for him. He didn't even finish searching the building. He took off.

Hearing the story piqued Tony's interest, but he also knew it was private property and didn't want to break in. Instead, he and several of his friends went to the porch of the old mansion, armed with a Ouija board.

"That was before I knew better about Ouija boards," he said with a laugh.

As they used the board, they began getting results, but then something even more horrifying happened. As they sat there in the moonlight, surrounded by the silence of the night, they heard a distinct noise come from inside the building. It almost sounded like a shuffle of feet on the old wooden floors.

They eased up from the porch, intent on looking through the windows. None of them had remembered to bring a flashlight, so they couldn't see anything.

"Hey, don't you have a lighter?" he asked one of his friends.

"Oh yeah," the friend said, fishing it out of his pocket. As soon as he flicked the lighter, they saw more than they bargained for. The curtains on the window yanked shut. It was as though ghostly hands had been holding them open.

"That made us want to leave," Tony told me. He and his friends took off in a hurry, making it his last visit to the mansion.

Robin Hill recently went through a full restoration, bringing the grande dame back to her original charm. At the time of this writing, the house is for sale.

I wonder what the woman on the balcony thinks about that.

HOVEY HOUSE

330 Walnut Street
Mount Vernon, Indiana

The imposing brick Italianate mansion consumes the entire corner of East Fourth and Walnut Streets, watchful and waiting. It's the kind of house that has witnessed so many lives, it's taken on a consciousness of its own.

It often draws your eye as you drive past. You don't always know why you have to look, but you always do. Maybe it's because something is also watching you from inside the dark windows.

The building in question has a celebrated history of being the home to Governor Alvin P. Hovey, who lived there from 1871 until his death in 1891. In his later years, he shared the house with his daughter Esther, along with her husband and children, who inherited the mansion after Hovey's death.

Hovey was an inspiration and a local hero. He was born in a log cabin just outside Mount Vernon and became an orphan at the age of fifteen when his widowed mother died. He continued to go to school but also worked on the family farm and took care of his sisters to keep the family together. He continued his studies, passing the bar when he was only twenty-two years old, and soon rose through the ranks. He served as a Circuit Court judge from 1851 until 1854 and as a Supreme Court judge for the following two years.

A current-day photo of the Hovey House.

When President Lincoln asked for volunteers to fight in the Civil War, Hovey quickly enlisted. He began as a colonel but was promoted to brevet major general by the end of the war. Afterward, he served as the U.S. minister to Peru for five years before returning to Mount Vernon to resume his law practice. He became a congressman in 1886 and finished out his illustrious career as the governor of Indiana from 1888 until his death in 1891.

The mansion was originally built by Richard Sullivan in 1845 and was sold twice before Hovey purchased it. It remained in Hovey's family until it was sold to the Masons in 1921, who replaced an addition with a much larger structure. By 1991, the six-thousand-square-foot building was in poor condition. Fearing it would be razed, it was purchased by the county and underwent $314,000 worth of restorations. It was soon utilized as official county offices.

Walking into it is a feast for the eyes. It embodies the opulence and grace of its period while remaining functional and practical. It has fifteen-foot doors on the main floor and an open staircase in the central hall. Gorgeous original medallions are on every ceiling, with beautiful woodwork through the building.

Above: The Hovey House circa 1921, when it was purchased by the Masons. *Courtesy of the Posey County Historical Society.*

Right: The grand staircase in the foyer of the Hovey House.

As I stood in the foyer, admiring the beauty, I could feel the spirits of the dead floating into the space. There were two of them. They were both female and were curious about me. It didn't surprise me that people have witnessed strange happenings at the mansion over the years. There were certainly enough ghosts there to maintain a respectable haunting.

I was there for a tour of the building. After trying to dig up ghost stories about the mansion for months, I finally hit the jackpot in a very big way. Not only was I getting a tour, but I was getting a tour from a Superior Court judge who had worked at the Hovey House for eight years when he was the Posey County prosecutor.

When Judge Travis Clowers showed up at the Hovey House, he was nothing like I expected. Maybe I thought he would be old and gray with the wisdom of age permeating from him like a fog. This man is nothing of the sort. While I'm sure he is as wise as they come, he is also young, charismatic and approachable. He could be your daughter's softball coach or the nice man at church who always holds the door open for you.

As he arrived, it was apparent he is well liked by the staff. They flooded out of their offices, happy to see him. He greeted me and my friend Traci Hoehn warmly and then took us on a tour of the building.

I've always adored old buildings, and there was a lot to love with this one. It was apparent it was built with careful hands. Every inch of woodwork was professionally handcrafted. No details were missed.

The bottom floor has several offices, along with a room for the County Council to meet. It reminded me of a mini courtroom, breaking away from the original intentions of the room. In another life, the room might have been a grand ballroom.

As we walked, Judge Clowers filled us in on the haunting.

When he first began working in the building, people were eager to tell him about the ghostly happenings. He didn't necessarily disbelieve the stories, but ghosts weren't his first thought when something unusual happened. Like most logical people, he always looked for a rational explanation.

One of the stories he heard came from Barb Vanzant, who was a legal assistant for the prosecutor's office for fifteen years before becoming a paralegal. One of her responsibilities was taking care of the files in the storage room. The storage room is a massive room with an eerie vibe. In decades past, it served as the Masonic temple. A stage occupies one end of the room, with a smaller stage on the opposite side. The middle is currently filled with file cabinets and boxes of documents. When she first started working there, nothing was organized, so she put everything in order.

Judge Travis Clowers when he was the Posey County prosecutor. *Courtesy of Judge Travis Clowers.*

She never felt uncomfortable in the building, despite the ghost stories, but she had a surprise one morning when she came in early. As she stood at her desk, she was startled to see the telephone light pop on. Someone in one of the upstairs rooms was using the phone.

"It was weird because I thought I was the only one there," she said.

With a sense of unease, she went to investigate.

The upstairs offices belong to the prosecuting attorney and the chief deputy prosecutor. The phone was located in a conference room that they refer to as the library room because of all the books lining the walls. The hair on the back of Barb's neck prickled as she approached the room. Who would be on the phone? What would she see when she turned the corner?

She walked in and stopped dead in her tracks. The phone was not merely off the hook; it was dangling beneath the table.

"I put my files on the table, said hello to Governor Hovey and went back downstairs," she told me with a laugh.

Her experience alone didn't prove a haunting. It was more about the accumulation of strange occurrences. Had it been the only odd instance, it would have been shrugged off without requiring an explanation, but it was just one of many.

Sarah Weber had a similar incident. As a legal assistant, she spent many hours in the office. One day as she sat at her desk working, she heard a thud come from overhead. Several others were in the office as well, and they all heard it.

She studied the ceiling for a moment. "I'm going to go see what that was," she told the others.

Directly above her office was the prosecutor's office, which was connected to the library room. As she climbed the stairs, she wasn't certain what she was going to find.

She edged around the doorway and then stopped short. One of the chairs was pushed out from the conference table and was sitting in the middle of the room, spinning in circles. The phone was also off the hook, dangling close to the floor. She stood there for a moment, trying to make sense of it. No one else was up there. Who had done that?

Finally, she gathered her courage and walked over, pushed the chair back in place and hung the phone up before retreating back to the safety of her office.

Other times, she felt the unmistakable sensation of someone walking up behind her. As she turned, there was never anyone there.

Theirs weren't the only experiences. As it turns out, the paranormal activity has been going on since the prosecutor's office first moved into the building twenty-eight years ago.

Back then, Child Support Operations also used the space. Lacking today's technology, they had to do all the tax offsets by hand, which was both time sensitive and time consuming. They were getting close to their deadline, so the administrator and her assistant stayed late one Friday night to try to push through and get it finished. They ordered pizza and kept working late into the night.

Near midnight, they were startled from their work when the phone rang. They looked at the phone and were surprised to see that the call was coming from one of the upstairs offices. They looked at each other.

"I thought we were alone in the building," the assistant said.

The administrator arched her eyebrows. "So did I," she said and then rose from her chair. She walked down the hallway to the foot of the stairs.

"Hey! We didn't realize someone was here. Who's up there?" she called up the stairs.

At that precise moment, the phone stopped ringing. She returned to the office and started gathering her things.

"Maybe it's time to go home," she said. She didn't get any complaints from her assistant. They knew when it was time to leave.

Glowers also had several experiences there over the years. When he was the prosecuting attorney, he often worked late into the night, especially when he was preparing for a big trial. The silence of the building would settle all around him, providing a blank canvas for the ghosts to work with.

As he was deep into his work, he'd often hear a strange sound. Sometimes it was difficult to identify the source. It was an old building that was prone to the normal creaks and groans. Other times, the sound was immediately identifiable.

One of these sounds was the automatic paper towel dispenser in the bathroom. In order to get a paper towel, you had to wave your hand under it to activate the motion sensor. He would hear it happily spitting out paper towel after paper towel. In the beginning, he got up to investigate and discovered his suspicions were correct. The dispenser had dispersed multiple paper towels, and he was the only one in the building. After a while, he simply ignored the noise, knowing its source.

Another strange sound he would often hear was the flushing of the toilet. It wasn't a partial flush, which some toilets are prone to doing. It was a full flush, as though someone had pressed down on the handle. He wouldn't hear it every time he worked. It only happened when the mansion was perfectly quiet, as though it was waiting for the perfect moment.

"The creepiest thing happened every time I was there," he told me. "I often went in at night. Sometimes it would be at one or two o'clock in the morning. If we had an officer working the midnight shift and they needed a search warrant to get into a house, I would go in and write the warrant so we could take it to a judge. Every time I was there, at some point, it was just time to leave," he said. "I would get my stuff and go. It didn't matter what I was working on. I'd leave."

The sensation was so strong; it wasn't a matter of choice. The ghosts of the mansion wanted the building back to themselves, and they weren't shy about asking.

One time, when he ignored the pull to leave, the situation quickly escalated.

His computer faced a wall, putting his back to the doorway. Even though it was closing in on midnight, he had several more things he needed to finish.

As he sat there, he suddenly felt someone come up behind him. The sensation was so strong, there was no doubt that a living, breathing human being had rushed into his office. He wheeled around quickly, thinking someone was trying to mess with him, but the doorway was empty.

The prosecutor's office where Judge Travis Clowers had several paranormal encounters.

"I packed up my stuff and was out of there," he said. "It was just very clear it was time for me to leave, and I didn't argue."

While I was there on my tour, I asked if Traci and I could do a short spirit box session in the Masonic temple room. Judge Clowers and Melissa Cartwright, who works in the building, walked upstairs with us but opted to remain in the library room. They weren't comfortable with what we were doing, something I understand. They both spend a lot of time in the building, especially Melissa, who actually works in the office where the child support administrator and her assistant had the strange experience. Drawing in ghosts and speaking to them might encourage them to hang around even more, something they weren't keen about.

A spirit box is a modified radio that scans rapidly through the channels, allowing the ghosts to talk through the white noise. In past experiences, I've found it to be a very effective way to speak with the dead. When it works, we'll often get full sentences answering our questions. When it doesn't work, it's just loud and irritating.

I turned on the device and also activated my digital voice recorder so I could record the entire session to play back later at home. Almost immediately, a male voice came through, saying, "Ben Emmitt Tuffley."

"Is that your name?" we asked.

We didn't get a response to our question, but another voice came through and said, "Hey, Ben!" as though he was greeting an old friend he hadn't seen in a while.

We asked a few more questions but didn't get anything interesting until the last question.

"Do you miss Travis being here?" Traci asked.

Without missing a beat, a male voice said, "Yes."

While I wasn't able to truly identify any of the ghosts, I also didn't feel like there were any negative entities there. More than likely, someone felt the same way I did about the mansion and decided to stick around.

I can't say I blame them. The Hovey House is a beautiful building, and I'm grateful to Posey County for bringing it back to its former glory.

I'm sure the ghosts are happy about this too—just as long as no one overstays their welcome and they all go home at a proper hour.

PART II

NEW HARMONY

I've always found New Harmony to be enchanting. Locals refer to it as "Utopia," which is an apt nickname. It very well could be heaven on earth.

When I was a child, my family would pass through it on our way to Mount Vernon. I'd press my face against the car window, trying to memorize every detail. The storefronts looked like something out of a fairy tale, each painted a different color with whimsical details. There were antique stores, a five and dime store, an authentic diner and several bookstores. Farther outside town, there was a labyrinth made of bushes with a tiny, mystical house in the middle. My younger sister and I always begged my parents to stop. On the rare occasion that they gave in to us, we'd race through the bushes, trying to beat each other to the center. My sister was small enough to climb through the bars on the door and walk inside the tiny house. She somehow always won the race.

I can also remember visiting my great-grandmother, who had a cottage not far from the Wabash River. The fireflies were always thick in that area. We'd race across the lawn, trying to catch them in jars, laughing without a care in the world.

Life goes on, as it usually does. I grew up, got married and moved a thousand miles away to Massachusetts. I raised two

New Harmony, current day.

children, divorced and then found myself at a crossroads. My kids were grown, with lives of their own, and I felt a little lost. That's when I packed up my pets and worldly possessions and moved back to my home state.

Friends and family members worked on finding me a home to purchase and couldn't understand why I was so fixated on New Harmony. They'd show me photos of cute houses in nearby Poseyville and Mount Vernon, but I wasn't interested. If I couldn't live in New Harmony, I wasn't coming back.

There was a reason for this, something I didn't realize at the time. New Harmony called to me, as it has done for many others. It has a way of collecting people, pulling them in with an invisible magnetism that is impossible to resist.

Soon after I settled into my new home, I explored the town and noticed something quite interesting. The entire town was haunted. As someone with mediumistic abilities, I could feel them in nearly every building. I had made a few friends by that time and asked them if the town was haunted. This was when I learned the reason why I was so drawn to the tiny town.

As a paranormal author, I felt this was the perfect place for me. It didn't take me long to begin collecting ghost stories. The first one was reported in 1868 when a woman passed a ghost on the staircase of an old house. More stories followed.

I quickly learned that the town has a fascinating history. It is the site of two former utopian societies. The first was founded in 1814 by a German Lutheran named Georg Rapp, who moved to the United States to escape religious persecution. After ten years, his group, fondly known as the Harmonists, sold the town to a Scottish man named Richard Owen, who made his mark on the town. While his utopia lasted for less than two years, his influence was long lasting. His progressive ideas about social reform, education and a love of the arts are embedded in every aspect of the small town.

Intrigued, I eventually wrote a book about the hauntings called *Haunted New Harmony* and then launched a ghost walk business there, something that has grown over the years. Six years later, I still live here and still marvel at how it came to be. The ghosts of New Harmony called to me, and thankfully, I was intuitive enough to listen.

THE BARRETT GATEHOUSE

Corner of Main and North Streets
New Harmony, Indiana

When the Harmonists first arrived at the area that would soon become their second utopian society, they had a lot of work to do. The twenty-seven-thousand-acre parcel of land they purchased was filled with swamps and forests. Before they could begin building, they needed to clear the land, drain the swamp and then begin setting up their lumber mill and brickyard. In the meantime though, they needed places to stay.

The Harmonists made quick work of the situation. As they began cutting down trees, they used them to build a series of temporary log houses. Many of them were crude but practical, and they served a purpose: they kept the members of the utopian society warm and dry. Once the Harmonists had the brickyard and lumber mill completed, they began tearing down the temporary structures so they could build more permanent housing on the same spot.

The Harmonists were industrious builders and were progressive in their methods. Many consider them to be the inventors of the prefab home. As the log houses came down, each new home was built exactly the same way. They numbered each piece of lumber, which would allow them to piece it all together once they reached the building site. This was quite an ingenious plan. If a portion of their house needed to be replaced at a later date, they could go to the lumber mill and get the specific piece they needed.

The Barrett Gatehouse, current day.

While most of the original log houses were demolished to make room for the newer buildings, several remain to this day. One of these buildings is the Barrett Gatehouse. By all accounts, it is the oldest house in New Harmony.

During the Harmonist period, the house was occupied by the J. Bentel family and originally sat on Church Street next door to the David Lenz home, which was eventually moved to another location. In current times, the land where it sat is located between Sara's Harmony Way and the United States Post Office. The two-story log house remained in its original spot until 1959, when it was donated to Jane Blaffer Owen.

Many consider Ms. Owen's time in New Harmony to be the third utopia. In 1941, she married Kenneth Dale Owen, who was a direct descendant of the original Owen family. He brought her to the town for a visit, and she fell in love with it. From that point forward, New Harmony would have a special place in her heart, and she forever altered the course of its history.

She brought charisma to the town in the form of spectacular parks, eclectic sculptures and, in some cases, a sense of quirkiness. By her direction, a roofless church was built to honor all denominations. People from all over the world come to visit the Roofless Church, taking in the sense of serenity and sanctity that abounds there. She and her husband rebuilt the crumbling granary, using grant money to invest $2.5 million into the project, and made it better than it was before. She built a stone labyrinth with a spectacular water feature, renovated many of the old buildings and breathed new life into a town that was quickly fading. She also rescued quite a few original Harmonist homes.

Her vision was to move the old houses to the street beside her beloved Roofless Church, creating a pocket of historic homes. When a local family donated the original house, she was elated. She named it the Barrett Gatehouse, after the couple who donated it, and set about moving it to its current location.

An old house and barn sat on the spot where she wanted to put the house, but she worked her magic and soon purchased the two lots and cleared the land. An addition was built onto the original structure, doubling the floor space. If you look closely on the west side of the building, you can still see the numbers the Harmonists carved into the boards.

For years, the house was used for visiting artists, writers, educators and friends of Ms. Owen, but in time, it became useful in another manner. Being a tremendous supporter of the arts, Ms. Owen built a pottery studio down the street. She created a grant program called the New Harmony Clay Project and invited select students to stay in New Harmony for several

The Barrett Gatehouse being moved to its new location. *Photo by Don Blair, used with permission by Workingmen's Institute.*

Left: A close-up of the numbered wood on the side of the Barrett Gatehouse.

Opposite: Donna Causland at work in the pottery studio.

months to work in the studio. At the end of their term, they would display their work at one of the art galleries before heading back home.

For the duration of their residency, they stayed at the Barrett Gatehouse. It was a perfect venue for the artists. The building had been modernized with a kitchen and bathrooms and provided ample sleeping space. It also came with an unexpected characteristic: the building was haunted. Nearly every resident had an experience they couldn't explain.

Donna Causland is one of these people. She is a straightforward, no-nonsense kind of person. Nothing rattles her, and she takes everything in stride. Originally from Cleveland, she now lives in Colorado and has completed two residencies as part of the New Harmony Clay Project.

During Donna's first residency in 2019, she stayed in what they called the Queen Room, which is one of the upstairs bedrooms in the original portion of the Barrett Gatehouse. At first glance, the Queen Room is quite pleasing. Sparse white walls define the space, giving it a sense of serenity. The furniture is timeworn and sturdy, practical and comfortable. But the room has a definite vibe. It's something you sense the second you cross over

the threshold. The energy in the room feels almost electrified, sizzling with current. It's the kind of sensation that causes the hairs on the back of your neck to stand at attention and makes you look over your shoulder to see if someone is standing directly behind you.

Donna would often see movement out of the corner of her eye. When she'd turn to fully look at the area, nothing would be there. It intrigued her but didn't frighten her. She soon came to understand that she wasn't alone, even if she couldn't see the other souls lingering there.

One area of the room that consistently drew her attention was the front corner where an old chair was parked. She used it as a place to put some of her clothes. She might hang a sweater on the back or place a pair of jeans she planned to wear again on the seat.

After she'd been staying there a few weeks, she began to notice a shift in the energy. Sometimes when she would catch movement in her peripheral vision, she would actually see her clothes falling onto the floor. It was as though they were pushed with invisible hands. She tried to find a rational explanation for the phenomenon but couldn't come up with one. The clothing that fell was always securely positioned on the chair. It was as though the ghost in the room didn't like the chair to be used for clothing.

During her second residency in 2021, she brought a thick comforter with her to make her room homier. It was quilted with air pockets. When

The Queen Room.

she sat on it, it made a distinctive sound as the air was expelled. The first night she stayed there had been a busy day. She'd spent most of the day driving and was eager for a good night's sleep. She tucked herself into her bed and was on the brink of falling asleep when she felt someone sit on the foot of the bed. The comforter made its normal sound. She opened her eyes and stared at the wall beside her, trying to make sense of what had just happened.

There was no doubt in her mind that someone had sat on the foot of the bed. While most people would have jumped up and raced out of the room, Donna took it in stride. She said, "Hi. I'm here now," and she closed her eyes and went to sleep. Nothing bothered her for the rest of the night. It was almost as though the introduction satisfied the ghost in the room.

Some weeks later, she walked into her room with the intent of getting ready to go on one of my Haunted New Harmony Ghost Walks. The shadows fell long against the hardwood floors, painting the floorboards with blackish shapes. It had been a busy day in the studio, but she was eager to go on the ghost walk. She'd heard about it from friends and wanted to see what it was all about.

She grabbed her coat from the back of the chair. As she put it on, she felt something jiggle in her pocket. She put her hand in her pocket, realizing there were several dog cookies in there from her dog at home. She scooped them out, intending to put them on the bed. As she did so, one of the cookies slipped out and rolled under the bed.

"Oh, I'll just get that later," she thought and then left for the event. When she returned later, she was stunned as she walked into her room. The small pile of dog cookies was still on her bed where she left it, but the cookie that had rolled under the bed was now in the middle of the room, centered in the middle of a thick prayer rug. It was more than three feet away from where it had rolled.

She stared at it for a moment, allowing the ramifications to fully take root in her mind. There was no doubt the cookie didn't move there on its own. It had been picked up and deposited there with a careful hand. She just shook her head and shrugged. If the ghosts were expecting an emotional reaction from her, they weren't going to get one.

Life as a pottery resident was often busy. Donna spent every waking moment in the pottery studio, retiring to the gatehouse late in the evening. One night, as she came home, exhausted but sated, she walked upstairs to her bedroom, wanting to put her phone on a charger.

Like many old buildings, there weren't many electrical outlets in the room. The only one that was accessible was the one behind the dresser. As she leaned over to pull out the dresser to reach the plug, she smelled a strong puff of orange. It was so strong and fragrant, it was as if someone peeled an orange right in her face.

She stood up, perplexed, and then began opening drawers to search for the source of the scent, but the drawers were all empty. She walked around the room, sniffing the air, trying to find the source of the smell, but it seemed to be contained to a small area surrounding the dresser. Then, as quickly as it happened, it disappeared.

She wondered if the smell was sent to her as a message. "Oranges were a special treat back then," she told me. "She must have given me that scent to let me know she was there."

She discussed it with another resident, a young woman named Katie, who surprised her by admitting that she'd experienced it, too, in another area of the house.

Donna wondered if it had anything to do with the doll she'd placed on top of the dresser. On her way to New Harmony several weeks earlier, she'd stopped by her mother's house for a quick visit. Her mother gave her an old doll that had once belonged to her grandmother. Donna was excited to have the doll and brought it with her to the gatehouse, putting it on the dresser for safe keeping.

She looked around the room, staring into the air.

"If that's you, this is my doll, and we don't play with her. The doll's name is Grace. You can come and look at her all you want, but don't touch her," she said. The message was apparently well received because the doll was never disturbed during her residency.

Donna never let the haunting bother her. She simply acknowledged the fact that she shared the space with an invisible roommate and went on with her day. Not everyone had the same reaction.

The ghosts at the Barrett Gatehouse must have been elated when Sydney Taylor Ewerth moved in. She was enthusiastic and bright, someone who livens up the room when she walks in. She drew the ghosts in like moths to a flame.

When she received the news that she was accepted for a residency at the New Harmony Clay Project, she had just completed her master's degree at the University of Alabama and had finished teaching her first semester there. Excited about the new adventure, she dropped everything and headed to New Harmony.

Becoming a part of the New Harmony Clay Project was a tremendous opportunity for aspiring potters. It gave them a chance to create pottery while living in a quaint historic town. Not only were they provided free lodging, but they were also paid to do what they loved best.

Sydney arrived in January, which is the quietest month of the year for the town. Many of the shops and restaurants are closed, leaving the town alone to itself. It's a time for reflection and solitude, but it also provides a great opportunity to create without distractions. After living in big cities all her life, Sydney was eager for a change of pace.

Initially, she loved the idea of rooming in the Barrett Gatehouse. Not only was it the oldest building in town, but it also had historical charm. She could walk through it and feel the history. Many of the rooms looked like they did back during the Harmonist period, with wide plank floors and low ceilings. The bedrooms were small but functional, and the space was perfect for its intention.

At face value, nothing should have given the building an oppressive vibe, but she felt it soon after moving in. She tried to shake it off, but she kept getting the overwhelming sensation that she was being watched, even when she was alone in the house. She tried to dismiss it, but the feeling persisted.

Several other pottery residents were also living there, so she was given the small first-floor bedroom. It was the only first-floor bedroom that was in the original part of the house. The room had nothing more than a twin-sized bed and a dresser but was all she needed. She wasn't there to camp out in the room; she was there to create pottery. She intended on spending as much time at the studio as possible.

As she walked in and parked her suitcase near the bed, she felt the strangest sensation. Somehow, the air felt heavier, as though it was charged with electricity. She looked around, trying to comprehend what she was feeling. Nothing seemed out of the ordinary. It was a simple room with practical furnishings.

The oddest thing she noted about the room was the old lock on the door. It was a hook and latch system that was unlike anything she'd ever seen before. It took some effort to get it to latch securely.

As the weeks passed, she made an effort to keep the door to her bedroom closed. It wasn't as though she had anything to hide, but the other residents had to walk past it to get to the upstairs bedrooms, and she didn't necessarily want them looking in her room as they passed.

Still though, no matter how careful she was to make sure the door was firmly latched, it wouldn't stay closed. She often came home to find the door wide open. She didn't think much about it until something truly strange happened.

Several weeks after she moved in, the guy she was dating came to visit. They'd spent a long day exploring New Harmony. By the time they retired for the night, they were both exhausted and fell asleep almost instantly. Hours later, Sydney was pulled abruptly from her dreams.

She sat up, trying to figure out what had woken her. She looked over and realized that her boyfriend was also awake. As they sat there, wiping the sleep out of their eyes, the bedroom door clicked and slowly swung open.

It was something directly out of a horror movie. She was so stunned; all she could do was watch as her heart nearly beat out of her chest. Normally, if the latch gave way, the door only opened an inch or two, but this time the door creaked all the way open.

"Is someone there?" she called out, hoping to hear a voice on the other side of the darkness.

In response, the door slowly closed and latched itself. It took them both a long time to get back to sleep afterward.

She tried not to let the strange happenings rattle her. The residency was a chance of a lifetime, and she refused to waste it by spending all of her downtime in terror. She talked with the other residents, who confessed to also having strange things happen to them, but oddly, none of them felt unsafe. They simply acknowledged that they were living in a haunted building and hoped the activity wouldn't get any worse.

It wasn't too bad when there were other residents living in the gatehouse. If something strange happened, she could always reach out to them. But their residencies seldom lined up, and she often found herself alone in the building.

She'd come in late in the evening, needing nothing more than a few hours of downtime before crashing for the night. These seemed to be the times when the paranormal activity was at its highest. Every sound seemed amplified in the stillness of the house, causing her to look over her shoulder.

When she found out one of her friends was going to be in the area, she invited him to stay with her for a few days. He'd never been to New Harmony before, so they spent the day walking around and taking in the sights. By evening, they were tired and retired to the living room to drink a few beers and catch up.

Even though she wanted to talk about it, she held back from sharing her stories with him. She wasn't sure where he stood on the concept of ghosts. Instead, they chatted about their lives and some of their shared experiences from the past. It was a welcome reprieve from her normal existence. By midnight, she had all but forgotten about the haunting—until something strange happened. As they sat there laughing and talking, they were startled out of their conversation by a loud rap on the door.

Sydney jumped up, not completely certain where the sound came from. There were three doors on the bottom floor that led outside. She walked to the kitchen door and opened it, seeing nothing more than the glow from the antique streetlights farther down the block.

She looked around, feeling the hairs on the back of her neck rise. New Harmony was a quiet town. The streets were almost always empty by midnight, even during the summer. The only sounds she heard were the crickets in the bushes. She closed the door and shook her head, trying not to get worked up by the interruption.

"Do you think it could be kids playing a prank?" her friend asked.

She took a tentative step outside and peered down the street, but she didn't see anything. Goosebumps broke out on her arms, and she rubbed them, willing them to go away.

"I don't think so. There really aren't very many kids in town," she said quietly, her mind spinning in several directions.

The sound was far too pronounced to be the normal noises of a settling house. It was definitely a deliberate knock. While she'd met a few people in town, none of them were prone to pranks. And like she'd told her friend, there weren't many kids in town. As far as she knew, no one would have a reason to scare her.

They returned to the living room and tried to resume their conversation, but as soon as they got comfortable, another knock sounded. This one was even louder than the first.

Her friend ran ahead of her to the front door and threw it open. He raced outside and looked around. If someone had been there, they wouldn't have been able to hide in the mere seconds it took him to get outside. No one was there. The town was eerily quiet, as usual.

They didn't hear any further sounds, but it had been enough to set Sydney's nerves on edge. What did they want? Why were they doing these things?

Several weeks after her friend left, he admitted to having a strange encounter of his own while he was there. One night, he had walked out onto the small patio to smoke a cigarette. As he was turning to come back inside, something caught his eye. A man was sitting on the roof of the building. The man was so lost in the shadows that it was difficult to get a clear view of him before he completely vanished into thin air. He tried to dismiss it as a trick of the eye, but the image had been so clear he had to wonder what he saw.

In retrospect, Sydney found it interesting. Nothing had happened in the house when other friends stopped by to visit, but her boyfriend and her friend both had strange experiences. Ironically, the two men had experienced near-death situations at some point in their lives. Her boyfriend became septic as a kid and was actually pronounced dead before they were able to revive him, while her friend had been in a horrible car accident when he was young and also died before being brought back. Both of them recalled seeing strange figures when they were dead. Did that open them up to having paranormal experiences? There was so much she didn't know, but she wasn't sure she wanted to find out.

All of these experiences were unnerving for Sydney. While she had a strong belief in the concept of an afterlife, she wasn't completely certain where she landed on the prospect of ghosts. She'd never had an experience prior to rooming at the gatehouse. The most that had happened to her was fairly trivial and easy to explain. After several family members passed away over the years, she sometimes had dreams about them, but it was nothing compared to the events that were currently transpiring. Some of the things that happened were almost explainable, but when they were put together, they painted a broader picture. The events felt almost deliberate, as though someone was trying to mess with her mind.

The haunting seemed to ebb and flow, like an ocean tide. For weeks, nothing would happen and the house felt normal, but as soon as she grew comfortable, all hell would break loose.

One day, after several weeks of normality, she was sitting on her bed with her laptop when the cover at the foot of her bed slowly slid off to the floor. She gasped as horror flooded through her system. Had it simply fallen off, or was it pulled by unseen hands?

She pushed the thoughts away, trying not to focus on them. She still had several weeks left in her residency, and she didn't want to spend it frightened. A week passed by quietly, and she'd nearly forgotten about the experience when something truly horrendous happened.

She awoke one night from a terrifying nightmare only to realize she was pinned to the bed. She was aware of the concept of sleep paralysis, but she'd never experienced it before. Was that what was happening? The only thing she could move was her eyes. Frantically, she looked around the room and was horrified to realize someone was standing at the foot of her bed.

It was a bare-chested young man. His face was mostly shadowed, but she could see enough details to know he was staring at her. Terror rose inside her as they locked eyes.

What would he do to her?

She couldn't even scream. Her body was paralyzed. All she could do was lay there helplessly and pray he would leave. After several long seconds, he faded away into the darkness, and she was freed from her paralysis.

She sat up in bed and turned on the light, frantically searching the room for any sign of him, but he was gone.

The following days were difficult to endure. She kept telling herself that she was just psyching herself up, that none of it was real. She tried to convince herself that the man in her room was nothing more than a bout of sleep paralysis and that all the sounds were just the settling of the old house. But while the words were enough to get her through her days, they weren't always potent enough to get her through the nights.

As soon as darkness fell and the town grew quiet, the house came alive. She'd hear a creak above her coming from an empty upstairs bedroom or hear the click of a doorknob turning. By the time she was approaching her last days at the gatehouse, she was completely on edge. Every sound made her jolt.

She worked tirelessly in the studio, but she still had two projects she needed to finish. Instead of leaving when her residency ended, she extended her stay for two more days. As much as she hated the thought of staying in the gatehouse any longer, she also knew she needed to leave with more finished pieces.

Everyone else had already gone back home, so she was once again alone in the house. After working in the studio all day, she came back one evening and decided to start cleaning and packing. The housekeepers would be coming soon to clean the house, and she wanted to leave it in good condition. She had food in the refrigerator she needed to dispose of and dishes in the sink she needed to wash.

Darkness was beginning to settle in. The last of the rosy sunset filled the windows and increased her anxiety. It would be full dark soon, and she wanted to be tucked in her room before the shadows got too deep.

She had her hands plunged into a sudsy sink full of dishes when she heard a loud bang. It almost sounded as though someone had jumped off a bed upstairs. She stood stock still.

"Is somebody here?" she called out, praying it was one of the housekeepers. The thought was unrealistic. If someone was there cleaning, she would have heard them. If nothing else, they would have called out to her when she came through the door. Everyone knew the gatehouse was haunted, even the housekeepers.

With trembling legs, she dried her hands on a kitchen towel and crept toward the stairs.

"Is anyone up there?" she called out again but got no answer.

Going upstairs was the last thing she wanted to do, but she needed to reassure herself that the house was empty. Thoughts of an intruder filled her mind with anxiety as she tiptoed up the stairs. When she got to the landing, she flipped on the hallway light and then peered into each room. No one was there.

With her heart thumping heavily in her chest, she hurried back downstairs, intent on finishing up quickly so she could start packing. As she turned the corner into the kitchen, she stopped short.

The patio door was wide open.

That was enough for her. She grabbed her purse off the counter and bolted from the building. She spent her final two nights with friends in town, only returning during the light of day to shove her belongings into boxes.

Sydney is now a professor at the University of Iowa, teaching ceramics. In retrospect, she cherishes the time she spent in New Harmony as a resident. It gave her the opportunity to explore her talents as a potter, but it also opened her up to the concept of the supernatural. While she believes that architecture can hold energy, she's also not eager to repeat the experience.

As Sydney left and the next round of residents arrived, I imagined the ghosts at the Barrett Gatehouse clapping their hands in glee. It's apparent they love interacting with the artists, some more than others.

If you ever find yourself in a similar situation, always remember to maintain your composure and realize that fear feeds them. It gives them the energy they require to continue scaring you. I know that's often easier said than done, but they have been there a very long time, and they aren't going anywhere. If you want to share their space, you have to play by their rules, whether you like it or not.

Red Geranium Restaurant

520 North Street
New Harmony, Indiana

I paused on the sidewalk, staring at the entrance to the restaurant. The last time I stood in that spot, I was a nervous seventeen-year-old on my way to bus tables at the exclusive restaurant. Four decades later, I was still nervous, but for a different reason.

I wasn't late to work or worried I would pour water into someone's white wine glass. I was apprehensive because the building was supposedly haunted.

What kind of haunting would I find inside there? Would it be a gentle haunting, like the ones I had witnessed in so many other New Harmony locations, or would it be something darker? The only way to find out was to push through the double doors.

I took a deep breath for courage and continued on. What I found was a pleasant surprise. The entry room was quaint and welcoming, with a grand piano in one corner and historic photos on the walls. It was a place with history and a sense of belonging in the tightknit community.

The Red Geranium opened in 1964, taking up occupancy in a building that was once a home. The previous owners were Ivan and Helen Stallings. Ivan was a carpenter and had a workshop in a building directly behind the property, in the area that is now the main dining room.

As I've discovered with other properties in New Harmony, the land had served many other purposes. According to an old Harmonist map of

The Red Geranium Restaurant, current day.

the town, called the Weingarten map, the location was once the site of a Harmonist home occupied by the U. Bentel family. The house was built circa 1820 and housed the Harmonist family until the group sold the town and moved back to Pennsylvania.

In the late 1800s and early 1900s, the property was a corn and wheat warehouse, owned by J.T. Stoper. Scales to measure the grain, as well as an office, were located beside the warehouses.

Next door to the building is another house known as the Green Gothic. It has green clapboard and tall Gothic windows, giving it all the charm and character you'd expect of an antique house in New Harmony. According to the *Posey County Interim Report: Indiana Historic Sites and Structures Inventory*, published in 1985, the house is known as the Pelham House, dated 1860, and is described as Gothic Revival. The two buildings are now connected, with the Green Gothic containing business offices.

The Pelham family has a long history in New Harmony, beginning when William Pelham joined the Owen community in 1825. He served as an editor for the *New Harmony Gazette*. His son, William C. Pelham, also moved to New Harmony, and his family became prominent in town. Although I couldn't find any documentation supporting the fact that they might have lived in the house, their family remained in New Harmony for generations.

I continued down the long, narrow hallway to the Grapevine Bar, where I met longtime server David Mayer. David began working at the Red Geranium in 1992 and has been there, on and off, ever since. He was warm and welcoming, and best of all, he was willing to share his stories. It wasn't long before I learned everything I would need to know about the paranormal happenings at the restaurant.

The restaurant has been haunted for years, with dozens of people witnessing the activity. According to David, one of the more common occurrences happens in the entry room. He brought me to the area where I had been admiring the piano and historic photos and pointed to the ceiling.

"There isn't a second floor, but we often hear people walking around up there," he told me. I stared up at the ceiling, wondering about the former layout of the building. Was it possible that the entry room once had a second floor?

He told me that many other people have also heard the footsteps. They sometimes also feel cold breezes, as though someone just brushed past them, and see strange shadows move across empty walls.

He brought me back into the bar to tell me the rest of his story. Besides the phantom footsteps, David has actually met the ghosts, up close and personal.

His first experience happened in the Green Gothic building. As he was making his way up the staircase to the second floor, he was baffled by what he saw at the top of the stairs. An older man stood there, watching him from the landing. "It looked like the image of an Owen. He had that body type, but I know it wasn't Mr. Owen," he said, referring to Kenneth Dale Owen, who was a frequent guest at the restaurant years ago.

Another employee was supposed to be following him up to the second floor, so David turned to look for him, to see if he had also witnessed it. Unfortunately, the employee hadn't reached the stairs yet, so he didn't see the apparition. When David turned back around, the man was gone. David quickly bound up the stairs and searched the small three-room space, finding it empty. Whoever had been at the top of the stairs had simply vanished into thin air.

Not long afterward, he had another experience that would leave him shaking his head in wonder. It happened in the main building, in the linen closet.

"I went upstairs to get some table linens and then went to turn the light off in the closet. It was a shotgun closet, so it was really long. I don't know what made me look, but as soon as I turned the light off, I looked to the very back," he said.

Even though the light was turned off, enough ambient lighting from the other room filtered in, giving him a clear view. What he saw was astounding.

The air in the closet was suddenly filled with a dusty mist, and then a woman appeared. Even though she was translucent, he could make out enough details to fully describe her. He said she appeared to be a Harmonist. She was a middle-aged woman with brown hair that she wore up in a bun. Her dress was long and dark and was accessorized with a white apron. She just stood there and stared at him with a blank expression until she disappeared. Could she be a member of the U. Bentel family from the Harmonist period?

If he thought that was his last encounter with the woman in the linen closet, he was wrong. Six years later, he would meet up with her again. He was closing the restaurant on a Saturday night. Everyone else was already gone, except for the overnight cleaning man. As David was leaving, he noticed the light was on in the upstairs office, so he went back inside to turn it off.

Everything appeared normal, so he assumed that someone had just mistakenly forgotten to turn off the light. Not thinking much about it, he turned the light to the automatic setting and turned to leave. Normally, the light stays on for fifteen seconds when it's in automatic mode before turning itself off. He pulled the door closed but didn't completely shut it. After he took one step down, the door slammed violently behind him and the light went off well before it was supposed to.

Without warning, he felt a strange tingly sensation. It ran from the top of his back to the bottoms of his legs, feeling like a surge of energy lacing through him. The energy suddenly pushed him forward, guiding him down

David Mayer going down the stairs where he was pushed.

the stairs. He couldn't have stopped if he tried. The momentum was so strong; all he could do was allow himself to be carried along like driftwood in a raging river. As he approached the hostess stand, he grabbed onto it and held on tight. Instantly, the tingling sensation evaporated and the pushing stopped.

He wasn't sure what had happened, but one thing was for certain. "She wanted me out of there," he said.

As if that wasn't enough, David had one last story to share with me. It's something that happens to him in the Grapevine Bar. The walls of the bar are filled with murals of grapevines and forest, giving it a quaint, cozy appearance. It's a quiet place to have a drink and relax.

Sometimes when David is standing at the bar, he sees someone peering around the doorway. "It happens every time I work in the bar," he said. "Sometimes four or five times a night, especially late at night after we're closed and I'm cleaning," he said.

Judy Smith also had several experiences at the Red Geranium during her twenty-two years of employment there. She, too, felt paranormal energy in the Green Gothic building.

One time, she was in an upstairs room that was formerly used for storage when she felt as though someone was behind her. The sensation was so strong, she couldn't help but react. "I turned around, and all I could see was a shadow move across the room," she told me. It was enough to prompt her out of the storage room and back downstairs.

After a while, she simply found a way to ignore the frequent sensations. Part of her ability to adapt came from her previous experience with the paranormal world. It wasn't her first involvement with a haunting. When she was a child, she lived in a house that was reported to be haunted. Her entire family would often hear footsteps and see shadows move. They also noticed items disappear and then reappear later. "You'd set your keys down on the table and they'd disappear. You'd look for them everywhere and then find them back on the table later," she said.

It made me wonder. People who are sensitive to spiritual energy often experience more paranormal activity than non-sensitive people. Ghosts have a way of knowing the difference and will often approach sensitives. If someone has had previous experiences, they are more open to the possibility of a haunting and are more inclined to have future encounters. When I asked David if he's had any other experiences, my theory fell like dust at my feet. His only experiences happened at the restaurant.

Other people have also experienced paranormal happenings at the restaurant. Judy told me that a former chef would sometimes feel someone tap him on the back. When he turned around, nobody would be there. People often hear other people walking through the kitchen when it's supposedly vacant. She also told me about the phantom footsteps in the entry room, as well as footsteps on the staircase.

The hotspots appeared to be in the Green Gothic building and upstairs in the office space.

The haunting isn't contained to the building either. Several people told me a story about a lady in white who has been spotted behind the restaurant. This was interesting to me because Judy also told me that the Harmonists used to have a brickyard in the area behind the restaurant. Were people seeing the Harmonists hard at work, or was it something else? The fact that it was a woman dressed in white made me believe it was something else since the Harmonists typically dressed in darker colors.

Was it connected to the story about the woman who drove her car into the river? During the 1970s, a woman and her two children were driving on former Highway 69 during a nighttime storm. She apparently missed the turn at the corner of Church and Main Streets and continued down Main Street past the restaurant. Currently, the road is blocked with metal posts to prevent cars from traveling down to the river, but the posts weren't there in the '70s. She drove all the way to the end, where the road meets up with the Wabash River. The storm was raging so heavily that she didn't notice the road ended at the edge of the river. Her car plunged into the water, and the three of them perished that fateful night. Could she be the source of the haunting?

I don't know, but I certainly hope not.

A part of me wonders if people are merely seeing the swans that swim in the lake behind the restaurant. If the moon hits the water in the right way, a swan could appear to be a misty shape that is moving in the darkness. I've visited the location numerous times at night, hoping to catch a glimpse of what people have told me, but I've been unsuccessful.

As I turned to leave the restaurant, I left with a happy heart. The Red Geranium is a beautiful, historic restaurant with outstanding food and an enveloping charisma. David doesn't feel as though there is any negative energy lingering at the restaurant. "It's just people like you and me who just decided to hang around." Maybe they like the food and the ambiance.

If you visit the restaurant, pay attention to the sounds you might hear in the entryway and the movements you might see in the doorway of the bar area. Even though there's nothing to be afraid of, that doesn't mean that souls from the past don't occasionally pop in for a visit at their favorite restaurant.

HAUNTED DOLLAR GENERAL

1119 Church Street
New Harmony, Indiana

Before I moved to New Harmony, people warned me there wasn't a grocery store in town. While there were two gas stations with convenience stores, true groceries were thirty minutes away in the neighboring city of Evansville.

Initially, it seemed like a small price to pay to live in Utopia. I would play a podcast on my car stereo, bring along a steaming cup of coffee and treat it like a weekly adventure. Over time, it became somewhat arduous, requiring too much planning. If you forgot something, you knew you had a half hour's drive ahead of you to retrieve it.

When rumors of a new Dollar General began circulating, opinions were mixed. Some of the purists didn't want a nationwide chain store mixed in with our two-hundred-year-old architecture, while others embraced the idea. A meeting was set up at our town library to hash out the details with the corporation. Locals came armed with photos, insisting that the company build something that would blend in with the town's historic charm. Others created petitions in an attempt to stop the construction.

Despite all the opinions, the Dollar General opened in the summer of 2019 and provided the small town with exactly what it needed. It was freshly stocked and well maintained. The staff there seemed to truly care about the appearance and selection and kept it in remarkable shape.

The New Harmony Dollar General.

The store was open for just over a year when the staff realized something strange was going on. Employees who worked the night shift often felt as though they were being watched. Items would sometimes fly off the shelves despite the fact that no one else was in the store. They talked about it among themselves but were hesitant to call it a haunting.

"How can it be haunted? It's a brand-new building," one store associate said.

This is something that happens more times than people realize. It was yet another case that followed the history of the land.

New Harmony was first settled in 1814, but the Harmonists weren't the first to stake a claim to the land. Nearly two thousand years ago, the Woodland Indians lived and hunted there. Evidence of their existence can be found in multiple locations, including several burial mound areas.

In more recent history, the land the building sat on was home to a barbecue restaurant. It burned to the ground nearly a decade earlier, and the land sat empty until Dollar General purchased it. Even though no one died in the fire, it doesn't necessarily eliminate the possibility of a haunting. People don't have to die on the property in order for the area to become haunted.

Sometimes ghosts simply drift in and are attracted to the location or to the people who spend time there. I've seen this happen time and time again. There isn't always a reason for the haunting and no clear-cut explanation for how it happened. In this case, I think it might have something to do with a nearby property.

When I began researching the history of the land, someone told me a story about the lot next door. Apparently, there was once a small shop at the front of the property with a trailer parked at the back edge. The man who lived in the trailer died of a fatal heart attack on the property. Could he be haunting the building?

During the summer of 2021, Julie Kimmel had something truly odd happen to her in the store, and she posted about it on Facebook. I saw her post and was quick to message her. She gave me a brief summary and then invited me to come down to the store at closing time so we could talk about it in more detail.

I waited until 9:30 p.m., knowing the store closed at 10:00 p.m. I didn't bring any of my paranormal gear. I just went in armed with my mediumship gifts. If something was there, I'd surely know about it.

Due to staffing issues, Julie was working by herself in the store. When I came in, she was putting away stock that had come in earlier in the day. She broke away with a smile when she saw me and shared her story.

"I don't like working here by myself at night," she admitted to me. "I hear things all the time, like things falling off shelves or footsteps when I know nobody else is in the store." She wrapped her arms around herself and shivered. "It gives me the creeps."

I couldn't say I blamed her. Even though I've spent years researching and investigating the paranormal, it's always a bit unnerving when it happens to you when you're all alone. You feel vulnerable. If something horrific happened, you are completely on your own with it. It was even more terrifying for someone who was afraid of ghosts.

"So what happened?" I asked her.

"It was crazy," she said, grinning, and then filled me in on the story.

Several nights earlier, she received a call from the alarm company, telling her that an indoor motion sensor had been triggered. She didn't think much of it because it had been happening almost every night. She pulled herself out of bed and drove down to meet the police at the store. After unlocking the door, the police walked around to make sure no one had attempted to break in. Everything was fine, so she locked up and went back home.

Julie Kimmel in the aisle of the haunted Dollar General.

The next morning, Luci Dunham, the store manager, checked the security camera footage and got the shock of her life. On the recording, a softball-sized ball of light traveled the length of one of the long aisles, made a U-turn and continued down another long aisle before zipping directly into the motion sensor. She couldn't believe what she saw. She tried to replay it, but the camera went dead and the recording disappeared. All she saw was static.

"Wow! That's so wild," I told Julie. I didn't want to take her away from the stock, so I asked her if it was okay for me to walk around on my own to see what I could pick up.

"Knock yourself out," she said, so I headed toward the back of the store.

I almost felt as though I was being pulled there by an invisible string. Soon, my ears began ringing, which is my way of knowing a ghost is near, so I followed the sound to the back aisle.

Once I tuned in, I began seeing a man in my mind's eye. He was tall with dark hair and a long black jacket. He was middle-aged and slightly overweight. He didn't appear to be negative, just agitated. As I stood there trying to pull more information about him, I also became aware of a little girl. She was around five or six and seemed quite playful. Was she the one knocking the items off the shelves? I could almost imagine her giggling behind her hand as she watched the store employees startle in fear. Movement caught my eye, and I turned to see an end display full of shower rods. One of the rods in the middle was swinging all by itself. Instead of swaying back and forth, it was actually swinging forward and backward. The experience stunned me but not enough to prevent me from pulling my cellphone out and recording it.

I stood there for a full four minutes, filming the moving rod until it just suddenly stopped.

"That was very cool!" I exclaimed. "What else can you do?" I asked.

I'm not sure if I shocked the ghost or thrilled her with my eagerness, but she didn't shy away from me. Seconds later, a large box fell from a shelf and landed with a plop on the floor.

"That's excellent!" I told her as I moved to put the box back on the shelf.

After speaking with Julie, I really wanted to talk to Luci, the store manager.

Luci has been the store manager since November 2020. Her first experience came as a surprise. She was sitting in the office one morning when she heard footsteps. "They came all the way up behind the counter and stopped at the door," she said. She knew she was in the store alone and was a bit unnerved by the sound. She got up from her chair and opened the door, finding nothing to explain the sounds she heard.

"Another time when it happened, it had been raining. The footsteps were squishy, like someone had wet shoes," she said.

I found this to be odd. I've heard phantom footsteps before but never any that corresponded with the weather. They were usually the same each time.

The store had just received their truckload of supplies for the week. They were busy trying to put it away, so I agreed to come back in a few days.

When I returned, Luci met me at the front counter. "It's funny because the store has been so active since you were here on Tuesday. Twice this week, we came in and the office lights were on. Today, we saw this," she said, pulling out her phone.

She showed me a video clip from the store's security camera. "Watch that clipboard," she said, pointing to the screen. As I watched, the clipboard did a slow pivot toward the wall.

"Wow!" I said.

"And there's no air movement going on in there. There's nothing that would cause it to move like that," she said.

Luci has had many other encounters in the store. One day when she was working, she heard a crash come from the back of the store. She rushed back to investigate and found a customer standing off to the side, looking at the shelf.

"It wasn't me. The shelf just fell over all by itself," the woman told her.

This didn't surprise Luci in the least. "Stuff like that happens all the time," she told me. "The other day, I looked at the security camera, and it looked like a big black hand was reaching down toward the party aisle," she said, pointing toward the aisle.

Knocking items off shelves seems to be the ghost's favorite pastime. Julie was working in the store one night and heard a crash come from the seasonal aisle.

"It's okay, I'll get it in a minute," Julie called out, thinking a customer must have dropped something. When she got to the aisle, she found a ceramic Santa broken on the floor. As she looked around, she realized there weren't any customers in the store.

Because I'm a frequent visitor to the store, I often stop and chat with the employees, asking if they've had any experiences. One young woman told me that she hadn't experienced anything, but she's heard plenty of stories. She said two employees were standing side by side at the front of the store one morning when they heard the distinct sound of a cooler door opening. They just looked at each other, knowing no one else was in the store.

"I don't want to experience anything," she told me, saying she often turns the radio up extra loud when she arrives in the morning to avoid hearing anything.

Another time I was in the store, I met a young man named Nick who was working at the register. He was eager to tell me about his encounters. He said the place becomes very eerie at night and that no one wants to work the night shift.

One night, he was closing the store. The doors were locked, and the store was empty. He was in the office doing paperwork when he heard someone come stomping up to the office door, just like Luci has experienced. Startled, he looked up at the security cameras but didn't see anyone outside the door. He got up from his chair and opened the door just to be sure, but no one was there.

Another night after they closed, he saw a dark shadow move down the aisle, heading toward the back door. He went back to check, but no one was there.

He said he's a little worried because now things are starting to happen at his house. Others have repeated this same fear. Nobody wants to bring the ghosts home for a field trip.

As I stood there talking to Julie and Luci, the stories kept coming. Nearly every person who works there has experienced something out of the ordinary.

"When you're here by yourself, it's a little scary," Julie said.

"But it's nothing compared to what happened to Kristy," Luci added, and the two shook their heads.

Apparently, Kristy was in the bathroom when she began seeing white lights bouncing on the wall in front of her. There wasn't much she could do about it at that moment. She was forced to just watch them until she was able to flee the bathroom. It's a compromised position to be in when something paranormal happens, and I feel badly for her.

"You come into the store in the morning and really look around," Luci said. But she also doesn't mind it. "I actually kind of like it. It's exciting," she told me.

While I was in the store talking to Luci, she introduced me to Brian Paris, who also works there. I've seen him in the store numerous times. He's always very polite and strikes me as a hard worker, something Luci attested to as we stood there.

Several days earlier, the two of them had been restocking the clothing area. Luci was handing Brian clothing, and he was putting it on the shelf. They heard something fall behind them. When they turned to look, they saw a small ball rolling back and forth on the floor.

This was astounding on several levels. For one thing, they had no idea where the ball came from. It hadn't been there when they started stocking the shelf, and the toy aisle was several aisles over from where they were. Secondly, the ball rolled back and forth. What they were seeing was impossible. It was as though two invisible children were sitting on the floor rolling the ball to one another. The entire encounter lasted for thirty to forty seconds and then just stopped dead.

Brian has also had experiences in the office. He's heard the same footsteps approach the office door, but he had something even more interesting happen. One day, he heard the sound and looked up at the security monitor in time to see a dark shadow walk away from the office door, moving toward the main doors of the store. When it got there, it met up with another dark shadow and disappeared.

"Sometimes when you're here by yourself, you'll hear things like this," he said, reaching up to rustle the potato chip bags. "It's like the ghost is trying to pick out what bag of chips it wants," he said with a laugh. He's also witnessed the front-door alarms going off, as though someone is walking through them, even when no one is there.

Intrigued by the constant paranormal activity at the Dollar General, we went in after the store closed one night with our paranormal equipment to see if the ghosts would talk to us. While I could feel them hovering around, they weren't very keen on speaking with us on the spirit box. The only clear answer we got came from a question Julie asked.

"Why do you always pick on me when I'm alone? Why can't you come out when other people are around?" she asked.

A male voice told her, "Funny."

Apparently, he enjoys scaring her, which wouldn't surprise me.

The spooky manifestations continue on a daily basis at the Dollar General. Some of the employees like it, and others could do without it.

"I don't like working by myself at night," Julie said.

I can't say I blame her.

PART III

POSEYVILLE

Poseyville is a typical small midwestern town with a strong sense of community. It has a quaint downtown area with buildings that have experienced many lives. The large store on the corner that used to be a big department store is now home to a physical therapist. The old dress shop is now a law office, and the water tower that sat at the end of Main Street was finally replaced, hitting a parked car as it was torn down. But some things have remained consistent. The grocery store hasn't changed much in the last fifty years, and the hardware store down the street is much the same.

Poseyville, Indiana, current day.

The town was founded in 1840 and was originally named Palestine. When they opened their post office, they had to change the name because the state of Indiana already had a town named Palestine.

My grandparents lived there for many years, and I have fond memories of visiting them. As a teenager, I went to high school just down the road at North Posey Senior High School and sometimes came to town to "go cruising" on a boring Saturday night.

Like everywhere else, Poseyville has its fair share of hauntings. People who become attached to their homes and businesses often have a difficult time leaving them behind.

Over the years, I've been asked to do several walk-throughs of homes the owners suspected were haunted. In each of the cases, they would hear footsteps when the house was otherwise unoccupied and would find objects in places they didn't belong. The hauntings weren't negative; they were just former homeowners who were still staking their claim to the property.

In one of the homes, the owners were doing a remodel of an older home. It's been my experience that renovations

The Poseyville water tower.

often bring out a haunting. If the ghost was someone who prided herself on the living room wallpaper and saw it being ripped down, she might have a thing or two to say about it. I always recommend talking to the ghosts of the house prior to any home projects. Just let them know what you're doing, whether you feel crazy doing it or not.

It wasn't until recently that I learned the town's public library was also haunted, as well as the local sports bar. I heard stories about an old laundromat that had ghostly activity, but I was never able to connect with the right people to check it out. I'm certain there are more ghosts hanging around, but small towns often like to keep their ghost stories to themselves. And that's fine, as long as the ghosts behave themselves. The haunting becomes much harder to dismiss once they don't.

Let's just hope that doesn't happen.

Poseyville Carnegie Public Library

55 South Cale Street
Poseyville, Indiana

L ibrary ghosts have always intrigued me. Imagine loving your job so much that you deny yourself a trip to heaven and go back to work instead. It happens more than you might imagine. Visit any old library and ask the head librarian if they have a ghost, and you might be surprised by the answer. Librarians are a dedicated group of people.

Such is the case with the Poseyville Carnegie Public Library. The first library was established in 1898 and was located in a section of an old opera house. It housed just over four hundred books.

In 1903, the growing library was moved to a room in the town hall, but it still wasn't sufficient. George Waters, a local banker, wrote to Andrew Carnegie, hoping for help in building a more permanent location. Andrew Carnegie was better known for his steel empire, but he also had a soft spot for libraries. For forty-six years, from 1883 to 1929, he provided grant funds to build 2,500 libraries nationwide.

Eager for a bigger library, Waters waited for as long as possible, but when he didn't receive a response from the Carnegie Corporation, he instigated a meeting with the tycoon. His efforts eventually paid off. The town received a $5,500 grant, doled out in three installments. The final $500 was provided at a later date to pay for library furniture.

Top: The Poseyville Carnegie Public Library, current day.

Bottom: The Poseyville Carnegie Library, circa 1905. *Courtesy of the Posey County Historical Society.*

Land was donated by Leroy Williams, and soon, a small Neoclassical Revival building was constructed on the site. After its dedication in 1905, the library was filled with nearly one thousand books. By the end of the year, nearly three hundred people had borrowed books from the new library. The Poseyville Carnegie Public Library was the smallest of the Carnegie

Libraries until 2000, when the library was expanded into the lot next door to provide a children's room.

The lot next door was once the site of a boardinghouse. Some say it had a rather ill repute. One person I spoke with referred to it as a house of prostitution. Regardless of what it was, the land, once again, played a larger role in the haunting.

Stories about the library's hauntings have endured for decades. Surprisingly, one of the primary ghosts isn't actually a librarian.

In February 2020, library director Heather Morlan was sitting at the library's information desk when she noticed someone coming through the front door on the security monitor. She recognized the woman as Linda Reising, their board of directors president, but she was surprised to see a young boy tagging along behind her. The boy appeared to be around ten years old and was wearing an old-fashioned blue jacket with the hood pulled up over his head. Heather jumped up, excited to see a child coming into the library. As she made her way around the desk, armed with candy and stickers, she didn't see the boy.

"Where's the boy?" she asked.

"What boy?" Linda asked, looking around her, wondering what Heather was talking about.

"I swear I saw a boy come through the door with you," she said and then described him. Remembering she saw it on the library's security camera, she ran back to the monitor to rewind the footage. To her astonishment, the boy had vanished. The screen was fuzzy in the places where he had been.

When Heather told her what she saw, Linda was visually startled. She had just returned from a trip to Oklahoma and had visited the grave of her father's younger brother. The boy died at a young age from asthma. Could it be the same boy? Did he follow her from the cemetery?

Linda showed Heather a photo of the boy, and the similarities were remarkable. It looked like the same boy, but what he did next made them wonder. Instead of following Linda back home, he remained at the library.

Silver Nelson, who has been employed at the library since 2019, has also witnessed him on the monitor. "One day, a woman came in, and there was a little boy with her. When she got inside, the boy disappeared," she said. "He likes to come in with families." Nearly everyone who works at the library has seen him from time to time, but the only place he's been spotted is near the front door.

There is another resident ghost that won't surprise most people. The Poseyville Carnegie Library also has a librarian ghost. While no one is

A memorial set up for Miss Carol inside the library.

absolutely certain about her identity, they are pretty sure it's Miss Carol. Miss Carol was a legend in Poseyville. She was the head librarian for forty-five years until she retired in 1997. Heather grew up in Poseyville and has fond memories of her.

"She walked around town with her pocketbook, hat and gloves. She had electricity at her house but no indoor plumbing. She heated her house with an old wood-burning stove that she also cooked on, and she chopped her own wood. She never drove. Her brother drove her into town and then brought her home every night," she told me.

Miss Carol was a true throwback to the elegance of the 1940s. She always dressed professionally, with a formal flair, wearing stylish hats and gloves when she went out in public. Her prim and proper mannerisms were also conveyed in the way she managed the library.

Before the addition was added, the library was divided into two sections. When you came into the entryway, there was a room to the right that housed adult books and a room to the left with children's books. "She wouldn't ever let me into the right side. She'd only let me into the left side where the children's books were," Heather told me, smiling. As a Sunday school teacher, Miss Carol was protective of her younger patrons.

After she retired in 1997, the library felt different. Everyone was so used to seeing Miss Carol sitting in her chair in the entryway behind the library counter; it seemed strange to see someone else in that spot.

Miss Carol retired to her small house on the outskirts of town and enjoyed her retirement. Unfortunately, it didn't last long. Miss Carol's life came to a tragic end on May 5, 2004. She was at home, chopping wood for her wood stove, when a drifter, looking for items to steal, walked through her unlocked front door. Miss Carol must have heard the commotion and walked through the back door, surprising him.

"What are you doing here?" she asked.

The intruder grabbed an axe that was propped up against the wall beside the door and violently attacked her until she was dead. The man was apprehended quickly and arrested. Due to a plea agreement, he was sentenced to seventy-five years in prison for the death of the seventy-nine-year-old librarian, something that didn't sit well with the town.

Her death hit the town hard and still resonates to this day. "Miss Carol was loved by everyone in town," Heather told me. "She never had an unkind word for anyone."

Soon after her death, her house was bulldozed, leaving nothing more than a long gravel lane. Life moved on, as it always does. The library continued to function, with new employees replacing those who left, but Miss Carol's stamp is still firmly on the library she loved so well. The new children's room is named in her honor, and a photo of her sits beside the doorway for all to see. And if her memory isn't enough, her presence is also frequently felt. Some feel that Miss Carol still lingers at the library.

Sometimes when they're working, the librarians will hear books shuffling on the shelf, as though someone is walking down the row straightening them. Silver told me that when she's working alone, sometimes books will get knocked off a cart that sits in the entranceway. "I just go pick up the book and put it somewhere else. I just figured Miss Carol didn't want it there," she said.

In years past, a rocking chair that Miss Carol used to sit in during story hour for the youngsters would begin rocking on its own accord. Patrons and employees witnessed it countless times.

The basement of the library also seems to be a paranormal hotspot. Heather was down there looking through boxes and heard the distinct sound of someone in the other room. It sounded like someone was shifting boxes and moving them around, despite the fact that all the lights were off. She was spooked by the noises and didn't walk into the other room to look. When she went back upstairs, she asked Silver if there was anyone else in the building, and she confirmed her suspicions. No one else was in the building—at least not anyone living. Others have experienced similar things, making the basement a creepy spot.

They also sometimes smell pipe smoke. The old part of the library sits on land that was once owned by a veterinarian. They tore his house down to build the library. And, not surprisingly to anyone, he frequently smoked a pipe.

I was curious about the haunting. As a medium, I could feel several ghosts roaming around the building, but I would need a quiet evening to really delve into the haunting. After I expressed interest in investigating the library, Heather agreed to allow us to conduct a paranormal investigation.

I was joined by Traci Hoehn, Rick Schlegelmilch and my friend Ben Adams. Heather and Silver Nelson also joined us, representing the library staff.

We started our investigation in the adult section. I feel it's important for us to introduce ourselves and let the ghosts know our intentions. I started it off.

"My name is Joni, and I come to you as a friend. We simply want to communicate with you and hear about your life. You know Heather, who is sitting next to me," I said. Knowing my process, Traci chimed in and introduced herself, followed by the others in the room. Once the introductions were made, I turned on my spirit box. As soon as I had it turned on, I asked them if they could introduce themselves. I immediately got a response. A man said, "I'm looking through it." It was immediately followed by a woman's voice that said, "Mable."

Before we could ask a question, the same woman came through with a nice compliment. "What great people!" she said with enthusiasm and warmth in her voice.

Rick asked if they ever read the books at night and leave them out. A male voice came through and said, "Ummm, no." The disdain in his voice was clear. It was as though he was telling us he'd never consider leaving a library book out on the table.

Silver was up next, and she asked if they had a favorite book. A woman's voice came through clearly. "Every one!" Her words made us laugh. Could there be a better place to spend your afterlife if you were a book lover?

We then focused our attention on the little boy, hoping to get him to talk to us and provide us with more information. Traci had brought a ball, so we placed it on the table. We asked a few questions but didn't get any clear responses, so we moved the ball to the floor where it was easier to access.

"There he is," Traci said. She was using my Structured Light Sensor (SLS) camera. It uses technology from the gaming industry that has been adapted for paranormal use. The device is quite phenomenal. It was originally developed for the X-Box Kinect system. It sends hundreds of tiny laser lights out in front of it, looking for human shapes. When it finds one, it maps it out and puts it up on the screen as a character.

Over time, people playing the games sometimes noticed an additional player on the screen when there was clearly no one else in the room. It wasn't long before paranormal investigators grew curious and began developing the software to suit their needs.

When we use the SLS camera, we point it in a specific area to look for activity. If there is a ghost in the frame, it will show up as a stick figure on the screen. I walked over to where Traci sat to see for myself. Sure enough, there was a small, child-sized figure sitting on the floor under the desk.

"Do you feel safe there?" I asked him.

Another voice came through and said, "Can you back up?" Apparently, I was too close for comfort.

The little boy simply would not talk to us, so I asked the other ghosts in the room what his name was. A female voice told us, "Jason."

"Can you tell me how old Jason is?" I asked.

"Eight," a female voice told me.

We investigated for another fifteen minutes, but my audio recording went blank for the remainder of the session, recording nothing but silence. We then moved into the children's room, which was built on the spot of the old boardinghouse.

I immediately began picking up on a young woman with long blond hair. She felt playful, as though she might pull pranks on the staff. I asked Heather

The children's area.

if anything ever happens in that room, and she laughed. "Just the lights," she told me. The security lights are on a timer to turn them on at night. The timer is in the closet, but someone keeps loosening the screws, preventing the timer from working. Heather has to go into the closet to screw it in tighter.

We decided to use our dowsing rods to get more information. These divination tools are simple to use and usually provide us with clear responses. We hold the L-shaped rods in each hand and ask the ghosts in the room to respond. We first ask the ghosts in the room to show us what *yes* looks like. In my case, the rods swing wide open. When I asked it what *no* looked like, the rods crossed. I then asked if she was the one who played with the security lights and the rods swung open, indicating "yes."

We ran the spirit box for a few minutes but didn't get any responses. I decided to turn it off but couldn't get the device off, no matter what I tried. Thankfully, I had my digital recorder turned on, because it caught an EVP. The voice, which whispered directly into my recorder, said, "The power!" It was as though she was trying to help me. And true to her words, when I pushed down on the power button one more time, the device turned off.

We moved to the basement where library associates often feel uncomfortable. Several times, while working downstairs, they would hear noises and see shadows in the back room. We turned on the spirit box and immediately got a hit. When we asked for their names, a female voice came through and said, "Emma."

Someone else asked if there was anyone down there who wanted to talk to us, and the same female voice said, "Not with your COVID." This was a fairly astounding response. With the world still dealing with the COVID-19 pandemic, this meant the ghosts in the building were aware of current events. Were they listening to the staff and patrons as they chatted about it during the day?

As the investigation continued, I kept feeling like there was a man down there. I saw him as a maintenance man who hung out in the back corner and didn't like anyone coming down there.

Someone asked if they liked it in the basement, and he came forward on the spirit box. "Go away," he told us, quite clearly.

After that, the spirit box provided no other voices. The choppy static sounds annoy me over time, so I turned it off and pulled out my dowsing rods.

We asked to talk to the man. We asked him a series of *yes* and *no* questions and learned that he took care of things. My impression of him was that he was a "man's man" from an earlier era.

Heather asked him if it was okay if she did a few repairs, and he responded, "No." Through further questioning, we learned that didn't like the fact that a woman was trying to fix things. He felt men should be doing the repairs. I could see Heather trying to suppress an eye roll. Like most women, she's come in contact with men like him before. Usually, though, they're alive and a bit easier to deal with. She assured him that she had men coming to do the manly work, and he seemed appeased by that. It was the last communication we would have for the night.

It's not unusual for the ghosts to simply shut down. I believe they run out of steam just like we do except on a bigger level. They also might grow weary of all our inane questions. It's probably a combination of the two.

We packed up our gear and thanked both the living and the dead for allowing us into their space and made our way into the night.

I'm certain the haunting at the library will continue. It's part of its legacy. Libraries aren't libraries without a ghost or two in residence. Luckily for the Poseyville Carnegie Library, it has at least three.

Ziggy's Pub and Restaurant

16 West Main Street
Poseyville, Indiana

L ooks can be deceiving in the paranormal realm. A building doesn't have to appear creepy to be haunted. If you drove down Main Street in Poseyville looking for a haunted house, you would drive right past Ziggy's Pub and Restaurant. The building couldn't possibly look more cheerful. It's painted bright blue to match the colors of the Indianapolis Colts football team, with huge white horseshoes and the team logo emblazoned on the front.

As usual, I understood the reasons behind the haunting once I researched the building's past. The building that Ziggy's Pub and Restaurant occupies has experienced quite a few incarnations. While it's been a bar and pub for the majority of its existence, it's also been a jewelry store, a five and dime store, a hardware store and a funeral home, which could account for much of the strange activity that happens there.

David Zickefoose, also known as Ziggy, bought the pub in 2006. When he began experiencing strange phenomena, it didn't surprise him. David is no stranger to ghosts. His grandmother was a psychic medium. She died when he was only sixteen years old, but she taught him one important lesson that has stuck with him over the years: trust your gut instincts.

After a close friend died in a car accident twenty years ago, he began seeing signs of his friend's presence. His young son's toys kept going off

Ziggy's Pub and Restaurant.

when no one else was in the room. One toy in particular seemed to be a favorite. He had a Bob the Builder toy that spoke phrases, and it continuously announced, "We can fix it! Yes, we can!"

Intrigued by the experience, David sat the toy in the middle of the room. "Brant, if that's you, make the toy go off," he said. It didn't take long before his friend complied, and the toy began speaking. It was a profound moment for David. Being able to connect to his friend was monumental to him. It let him know that Brant was still there in spirit.

David is also prone to having premonitions, something he's experienced most of his life. "It's really strange. I'll be thinking about someone, and they'll walk into the bar," he said. He had a customer who used to come in frequently, but months had passed since he'd last seen him. He mentioned it to his wife, and then the man walked in the door the next day.

Before David purchased the building, it already had a long history as a bar and restaurant. For decades, it was known as the Playhouse. Originally, the kitchen was on the right side of the building, but after a fire nearly destroyed the building in 2015, David moved the kitchen to the left side when he rebuilt. Before the fire, they would often hear strange noises coming from

A 1948 photo of the bar that would one day become Ziggy's Pub and Restaurant. *Courtesy of David Zickefoose.*

the kitchen. It almost sounded like someone was flinging ice from the ice machine across the counter and floor. When they would go in to investigate, nothing was out of place. Sometimes, it sounded like someone was back there banging pots and pans as they were cooking.

Intrigued, David brought in several friends who were paranormal investigators. They conducted a spirit box session and immediately heard the name "Carl" come across the device. David later learned that a man named Carl was one of the original bartenders when the building was first constructed.

The spirit box kept saying, "The wall." It didn't take much thought to understand what Carl was trying to tell them: a photo of him hangs on the wall in the bar. They weren't able to learn anything else about Carl or his reasons for remaining at the bar. More than likely, the bar held happy memories for him, and he decided to spend his afterlife there.

Not surprisingly, the building was haunted long before it changed ownership. Years earlier when the bar was still known as the Playhouse, the employees there also had odd paranormal encounters.

Michele Wilkerson worked at the Playhouse for over ten years and also experienced the haunting firsthand. The basement was always a hotspot for her. When she needed to change the soft drink canisters, she had to go into the dark depths of the basement. Something about the back corner always creeped her out. "I always felt like someone was watching me," she said. She'd race down, spending as little time down there as possible. The space was cold and damp, feeling darker than it should have. She always brought a flashlight for when she thought she saw something move in the shadows, but by the time she looked, it was long gone. Once when she was down there, she felt fingertips brush the back of her neck. It was enough to send her running.

When David gave me a tour of the basement, he told me something fairly startling. There were two reasons why the basement was haunted. First, when the building was used as a funeral home, they did all the embalmings in the basement. He even showed me the concrete ramp that they used to bring the bodies in from the hearse.

The second reason had more to do with entertainment. Years ago, men in the area used the basement for high-stakes card games. People from all over the county would participate. A psychic medium David brought in told him there was an angry man there, something I also felt. Had he lost his fortune during a card game and was hoping to get it back? Or was he a lost soul from the funeral home days? Sometimes, it's impossible to know unless the dead choose to speak with us. They tried several spirit box sessions in the basement, but the man said very little.

One of the upstairs bathrooms is also notoriously haunted. For years, women would complain about feeling watched while they were in the ladies' room. Many women made it a point to use another, less convenient bathroom just to avoid going in there. One day, Michele was sitting at the bar taking a break when a waitress named Vicky came rushing in.

"I need a drink!" she said, visibly shaken.

"What's the matter?" Michele asked.

It took the woman a moment to compose herself. "I walked to the bathroom and reached around the doorframe to turn the light on, and a cold hand ran right up my arm!"

The experience was terrifying for her. While she didn't actually see the hand, the sensation was undeniable. Michele said that other women had similar experiences. "Nobody liked that bathroom," she said.

Not knowing about Michele's story, David told me stories of his own about that same bathroom. "I'm always finding the water turned on. I'll walk in and shut it off and then find it turned back on an hour later," he said.

Michele remembers a time when they needed an electrician to do some work in the kitchen. She could hear him back there working, but it wasn't long before he pushed past her. "I'm not coming back until someone can be here with me," he said. Something had scared him to death, but he wouldn't talk about it.

Michele also remembers seeing something strange in the mirror that used to hang over the back bar. "If you'd stand there counting your cash, you could look up and see a lady walking through the bar behind you," she said, describing the woman as having dark hair and a long white Victorian-style dress. "I'll just count the cash tomorrow," Michele's manager said one night and took off for the door.

I mentioned this to David. While he hasn't witnessed it personally, he said that quite a few other people have experienced it over the years. "They've seen her mostly in the basement," he told me. They have no idea why she's there or what business she was attached to. The woman never interacts with anyone. She just floats through the room and then vanishes.

The paranormal happenings are continual. One day, David was sitting at the bar and felt someone tap him on the shoulder. He turned, thinking it was a friend trying to get his attention, but no one was there.

A friend of his had a similar experience while sitting at the bar. Instead of getting a tap on the shoulder, someone or something tugged on his jacket. He whipped around to look, but nobody was there.

One of the more frequent encounters David has experienced came one day as he was behind the bar working. He used to have a security camera set up in the dining room with the monitor mounted on the wall beside the bar so he could see if someone came in the other door. He heard a loud thump and then saw that the monitor screen went to static. When he came around from behind the bar, he realized the reason for the scenario. Someone had yanked the electrical plug connected to the monitor out of the wall. It was a heavy plug and was securely plugged into the wall. And even more troubling, the cord was pulled out to its full length, as though it had been tugged from the wall by an unseen hand. David plugged it back in and started to walk back to the bar when he got a nudge to go check the bathroom. Sure enough, when he turned on the light, he saw the water was running. He turned it off and walked back to the bar just in time to see the electrical plug launch itself back out of the wall. It was apparent someone didn't want him to see what was going on in the dining room.

As we sat at the bar chatting, more stories came to him. "Oh, did I tell you about the ice scoop flying across the room?" he asked. I shook my

The bar area of Ziggy's where much of the paranormal activity occurs.

head, so he continued. "Back when the kitchen was over on the other side, I was walking through and something went flying past me," he said. The noise was startling, but David seldom gets rattled over anything he experiences at the pub. He turned to look and saw a big metal ice scoop sitting on the rug. It had flown over fifteen feet to crash into the wall in front of him. It was probably a good thing the ghost has poor aim or David might have been injured.

"Anything else?" I asked.

David smiled and shook his head. "It's just all the time. We never know when something is going to happen," he said.

If you venture into Ziggy's Pub and Restaurant, I highly recommend getting the Ziggy Burger. It's made with fresh ground beef and comes with a toasted bun and a side of delicious French fries. If you feel someone tap you on the shoulder while you're eating, that's just a bonus experience.

David has invited me back to investigate the bar at a later date. My hope is to learn more about the ghosts that linger there and possibly help a few of them find their way to peace.

PART IV

OTHER TOWNSHIPS AND UNINCORPORATED COMMUNITIES

If you meander around Posey County with no destination in mind, you might pass through several of the other townships and unincorporated communities that tie this county together. Many of them are small burgs with a handful of homes. Some have the added benefit of having small businesses, but most are nothing more than acres upon acres of land with a few houses dotting the landscape.

The unincorporated town of Solitude is a good example. If you drove through today, you'd see a few houses along the highway. What you wouldn't see is the old general store that once sat next to Big Creek. I remember going in there with my grandpa and marveling at the creaky wooden floors and the old-fashioned soft drink machine near the door. Old men would sit on the front porch, talking about the price of grain and rehashing old memories from the past. There was always a friendly dog as well, offering a head to scratch as you walked past. The store was torn down years ago, but I'm sure the land still remembers all the lives that passed through that spot.

Another town would be Oliver. My stepmother, Susie, grew up there. Her family owned the general store that is

Welcome to Griffin.

now nothing more than a memory. I remember getting my very first Push-Up there, delighting at the creamy, orange-flavored ice cream that always dripped down my knuckles.

Some of the buildings in these places hold a deep, dark secret. It reminds us that hauntings don't follow a blueprint. All it takes is a will to remain earthbound following death. A tragedy isn't even required in the list of ingredients. Sometimes it's as simple as an old woman wanting to check on her beloved cows.

Some of the hauntings are obvious, but others are more reclusive and are tucked away under the façade of everyday life. It's enough to make you take a second look at the community you live in. If there are ghosts here, there could also be ghosts in yours.

GREATHOUSE SCHOOL

Undisclosed address
Point Township, Indiana

T imothy and his boyfriend, Jake, were out for a Sunday drive. As they drove, something caught Timothy's attention on the side of the road. It looked like an abandoned building. He did a U-turn and headed back to the spot where he saw the building, parking in a swatch of winter brown grass. The two men got out of the car to get a better look. What they found astounded them. It was an old schoolhouse.

It sat beside the county road, hidden from plain view by a bank of evergreens. While it had been built with loftier purposes and had spent many years filled with happy, laughing children, it had fallen onto hard times. It now sat in the shadows, watching the world pass by through the gaps in the trees.

Built in 1913, the Greathouse School was constructed of cinder blocks and wood, replacing a wooden structure built on the same site in 1872. The building was named after James Madison Greathouse, who was a township trustee in Point Township, located just outside the Mount Vernon town line.

If you look at a map of Indiana, Point Township is easy to find. It is the southernmost tip of the state, its shape defined by two rivers: the Ohio River, which runs along the bottom of the state, and the Wabash River, which separates Indiana from Illinois to the west.

Above: The Greathouse School as it stands today.

Opposite: An open window.

The school itself was a humble structure, built with admirable intent. Point Township was a rural area, filled with farmland that was susceptible to flooding. Children in the area would have had very little opportunity for education before the school was built.

The one-room schoolhouse was quickly filled with students who were taught by one teacher. The school lasted for nearly twenty years before it was closed in 1932, with the students being relocated to other nearby schools.

In 1937, the now-vacant school building was rented to a man who kept horses, hogs and dogs on the property. After becoming somewhat of a nuisance and seldom paying rent, he was asked to leave the property. The Dixons, who owned the building, then sectioned off the one-room schoolhouse into four rooms and used it as living quarters for their farmhands, despite the fact that it never had running water or electricity. The last renter left in the 1970s, leaving the building vacant.

Despite its proximity to the county road, the building was virtually untouched by human hands for many decades. If you were brave enough to take a look inside, it almost appeared as though the last occupant fled in the

middle of the night, leaving behind a bounty of possessions that eventually rotted where they fell.

Most of the locals avoided the property because of the uneasiness that came over them when they approached the old school. They felt as though someone was watching them. Some reported seeing faces in the windows that disappeared in the blink of the eye. The sheriff's department was called out frequently because people reported seeing lights in the windows. When they'd arrive, they'd see a handful of young people scurrying out of the windows after a night filled with ghost hunting.

Unlike many old abandoned buildings, this one wasn't adorned with graffiti, and none of the cast-off artifacts had been removed. It was like a time capsule. It was also ripe for a haunting.

Behind the property was an old paupers' cemetery. People who couldn't afford proper burials were laid to rest there. Most of them were farmhands or dock workers from nearby Mount Vernon. While not all cemeteries are haunted, some still have energy attached to them. It was entirely possible that lost souls who were wandering the cemetery found some comfort in the old abandoned school and took up residence there.

Occasionally, someone drove past the old school and stopped to get a closer look. Most walked around the exterior of the building, took some pictures and then left. Very few actually went inside. Not only would they be trespassing, but they also subconsciously knew they might get more than they bargained for. If they weren't arrested, they might find themselves confronted by an angry ghost.

Timothy wasn't one of these people.

Dark-haired and handsome, Timothy seldom looked for trouble. He was raised in a good family and avoided the party scene that many of his acquaintances seemed to enjoy. Timothy was more interested in satisfying his curiosity about the unknown. As a child, he grew up in a haunted house, and thoughts about it followed him into his early twenties. He was always looking for opportunities to learn more about the supernatural world that had terrorized him as a child. Finding the old schoolhouse was a dream come true.

As he and his boyfriend picked their way through the overgrowth, Timothy began getting a bad feeling. Something wasn't right about the building. The closer he got, the stronger the feeling grew.

"Maybe this isn't a good idea," he said, but Jake was too far ahead of him to hear his words. He thought about catching up with him and turning back, but something stopped him. He'd waited half his life for an opportunity like this, and he wasn't going to back down just because it gave him bad vibes.

Many of the windows had been boarded up, but several were open to the elements. It wasn't difficult to imagine ghosts of the past staring back at them through the dark, maw-like openings. They walked around the building, trying to make sense of it.

The Greathouse School in its earlier days. *Courtesy of the Posey County Historical Society.*

"It looks like an old school," Timothy said, craning his neck to get a better look at the old bell tower.

"That's because it is an old school. There's a sign up there," Jake said from around the corner. Timothy joined him and looked up at the old sign.

"Greathouse School. It was built in 1913."

As Timothy stood there, he could easily imagine what the school must have looked like when it was freshly built. The sounds of children's voices would have filtered through the open windows, interrupted by the stern voice of the teacher, trying to reel in her students.

Fully intrigued by the building, the two retraced their steps back to an open window in the basement. They knelt down and peered through the opening, seeing rusty artifacts from the school's early years. They knew they shouldn't go inside, but the temptation was far too great.

With anxious glances over their shoulders, they slipped through the window and found themselves in a partially flooded basement. Timothy noticed a set of stairs off to the left. One of the stairs was missing a step, but he easily climbed over it and found his way to the first floor. Jake came up behind him, and the two just stood there for a moment and marveled at what they'd found. It was like stepping back in time.

The room just off the stairs looked like a kitchen. An ancient stove rested against one wall, with other relics from the school's century-old history littering the floor around it. Timothy could see old pans, a dented toaster, metal legs from antique schoolhouse desks and an assortment of other remnants.

Two other rooms branched off the kitchen. One was a room with an old orange recliner with mouse-chewed holes all over it and a kitchen table that was remarkably still standing. At the far end of the room stood a wood-burning stove with the door open, waiting to be filled.

The other room was nearly lost in dark shadows. Jake pulled out his flashlight and beamed it into the room, not wanting to take a chance on the old floors. As his light landed on something inside the room, both men gasped.

It was a dead animal. At first, they both thought it was a dead dog, but upon later evaluation, they realized it was a raccoon that had been mummified by time. It was enough to send them both retreating back to the kitchen.

The minute they reached the kitchen, something odd happened. They both heard footsteps in the room behind them. They turned to look, and the world went black. The next thing they knew, two hours had passed by. The sun had set, and the room was completely dark.

As Timothy snapped out of the apparent fugue that had come over him, he looked down at his phone and realized what had happened. He nudged Jake, who was standing beside him. He looked like he was sleeping with his eyes open.

"What just happened?" Jake said, as his eyes slowly refocused. He looked down at his phone. "It's been two hours. Do you remember anything?"

Timothy shook his head. "Not a thing. We need to get the hell out of here," he said, heading swiftly for the door to the basement.

It didn't take them long to get back outside. A sharp wind blew through the bare trees, chilling them both to the bone. They raced through the thorny woods and made it to their car.

On the way home, Timothy began seeing visions in his mind. He saw a dark-haired man who was dressed in an old-fashioned suit with a bowler hat standing in front of the old school, except it wasn't old in his vision. The school was new and fresh. Children poured in the door, and the man smiled, greeting them as they passed him.

Timothy couldn't stop thinking about the old school for days. He returned to Mount Vernon and visited the local library but couldn't find very much information. All he found was a long framed photo of a group of people. Handwriting along the bottom identified the photo as members of the Greathouse family. As he looked down the row of people, his eyes stopped at one man. The man was wearing an old-fashioned suit and a bowler hat. This was the man from his vision.

Obsessed with thoughts about the old school and the experiences they'd had there, Timothy and Jake returned several days later with their friends Mia and Ava. Mia and Ava are identical twins, which was interesting because Timothy also has an identical twin. Both women were in their early twenties and were fair haired and intuitive. Of the two, Mia seemed to be more in tune with her metaphysical abilities. Timothy often used her as a sounding board when he ran into something paranormal.

Mia's reaction to the old school was surprising though. She found the old schoolhouse to be warm and inviting. She didn't feel any malice whatsoever.

Ava's experience was dramatically different. After being inside the schoolhouse for a few minutes, she heard someone whisper in her ear, a sound that sent her running. Jake went outside with her and kept her company while Timothy and Mia investigated.

They had a digital recorder and began doing an EVP session, hoping to catch ghost voices on the device. As the silence settled around them, they heard a dog bark. It sounded like it was close. This was a bit unnerving to Timothy because it made him wonder if someone was walking a dog nearby. After the barking stopped, they both became aware of the sound of a clock ticking.

"Do you hear that?" he asked.

Ava nodded. "It sounds like an old-fashioned clock."

They decided to review their audio. When they got to the places where they heard the dog barking and the clock ticking, the recorder was silent. It hadn't recorded the sounds both of them heard. But they did hear something else that was absolutely spine chilling.

When Timothy asked them what their names were, they got three responses. One was difficult to make out, but the other two were abundantly clear. One whispered the name, "Tina." The other voice screamed with a roar. "George Sampson!" it said.

They weren't the only ones having a strange experience. While Jake and Ava waited outside, Jake took a picture through the basement window. When he looked at his screen, he jolted. It looked like there was a glowing red figure on the other side of the window. Startled, they rushed inside to tell Timothy and Mia. They found them in the basement doing an EVP session.

Was the entity from the photo standing there beside them? The thought was appropriately chilling.

In a typical EVP session, the responses aren't audible. You have to play back the recording to hear them on the digital recorder. They asked a few questions and then listened to what they'd recorded. As soon as they pressed the play button, they heard Timothy's voice come through.

"Who's down here?" he asked.

The response was instantaneous. "F--- you, Timothy!" it said.

"Do you want us to leave?" they heard Ava ask.

The response was clear. "Let's go," it said.

It gave them all goosebumps. "We're leaving, but you can't go with us," Timothy said adamantly. None of them wanted to bring a ghost home with them. Just the thought made Timothy shudder.

Timothy had a difficult time containing his excitement over the experience they'd had there. After a decade of watching paranormal television shows, he was elated to finally find himself in the thick of things instead of watching others on TV. He also realized that investigating the paranormal came with a price. Something could very easily follow you home, and that was something he wasn't comfortable with.

A month later, Timothy ended up back at the old school. His friend Jared wanted to see the school, but Timothy had his concerns. Jared had a tendency to be edgy and sometimes experimented with dark witchcraft. After hearing the EVP, Jared laughed and told them he was going to invite the ghost to come home with him so he could experiment with it.

"That's really not a good idea," Timothy tried to tell his friend, but Jared couldn't be swayed.

After his previous encounters, Timothy was hesitant to go onto the property. Jared had no problem going in alone, so they dropped him off and drove down the road a few miles and waited.

After a half hour, Timothy grew concerned. "Maybe we should drive by and make sure he's okay," he suggested.

"Fine, but we're not going inside," Jake stated emphatically.

They started the car and drove back, coasting slowly as they went past the bank of trees. What they saw left them both shaken. Jared was walking at the edge of the property, but something was horribly wrong with him. His eyes were unfocused, and he almost seemed to be glowing. They tried to talk to him, but he vanished into the bushes, so they drove farther down the road. A half hour later, they came back, too worried to leave him there any longer.

They found him waiting beside the road. He had a fresh cut on his face and seemed very out of sorts. He said he blacked out the minute he got upstairs and didn't remember anything until they picked him up. They took him home and dropped him off. They haven't seen him since.

Jared's social media paints a very clear picture. Shortly after his experience at the old schoolhouse, his life took a dark turn. He began taking drugs and hanging around with people who were bad influences. Timothy believes that Jared brought the ghosts home with him, something that would impact his life for years.

If you feel compelled to search for the old Greathouse School, just know that it comes with a heavy price. Not only will you be trespassing and possibly charged with a crime, but you could end up with more than you bargained for.

The ghosts of the Greathouse School don't want visitors, and they will make sure you are punished.

THE HAUNTING OF GRANNY SCHNAUTZ

Denzer Road
St. Phillips, Indiana

Sheila grew up on Denzer Road in the St. Phillips area. Denzer Road is a rural, two-lane road that winds through forests and fields with a scattering of homes along either side. It's the kind of area that allows residents some measure of privacy, while remaining close to civilization and all the conveniences it offers. For Sheila, it was an idyllic place to grow up.

It was the kind of community where everyone knew everyone else. When an EF-1 tornado touched down in the area in 2016, toppling trees and damaging homes, everyone pitched in to help one another. "It wasn't very much fun, but nobody got hurt. We have great neighbors who are cleaning up for us, so that's about all you can do," one resident said on a WFIE Channel 14 news report.

As children, Sheila and her brother ran all over the neighborhood, but one of their favorite places to go was the Schnautz house. The Schnautzes lived down a long lane. They had a modest farmhouse and a large barn where the family kept their dairy cows. Sheila and her brother loved to visit the farm, mostly to see Granny Schnautz.

Granny Schnautz was an unusual character. She always dressed in old-fashioned outfits with a bonnet and pinafore apron. She never wore pants, always favoring long skirts that brushed the ground. When the kids came by, she was always happy to see them. She gave them oatmeal cookies and let them feed her enormous cows. It wasn't unusual to see Granny out looking for her cows. They had a tendency to break through their fence on a regular basis. Sometimes the neighbors would pitch in to help her, knowing how much her cows meant to her.

After Sheila grew up and got married, she ended up moving back to Denzer Road. Her parents lived just down the road from them, which was an added benefit.

One Sunday night, she happened to look out her window and saw the lights on at her parents' house. She knew they were at church, so she took a better look and noticed her brother's truck in their driveway. It wasn't unusual for him to drop by, so she decided to walk down to visit with him.

It wasn't quite dark. The sun was perched on the horizon, sending dark shadows across the road. As she passed the oil tanks on the edge of the road near the turn-off to her parents' house, something caught her eye. Granny Schnautz was standing at the end of her lane.

"She doesn't need to be out here this late at night," she commented to herself, wondering if one of Granny's cows had gotten out. It was something that happened frequently, so she didn't think much of it beyond the fact that the eighty-year-old woman might need some help considering how dark it was getting.

"Hey, Granny!" she called.

The old woman turned and looked at her before heading down the lane and walking back toward her house. Her behavior was odd; she was normally very friendly.

Sheila was eight months pregnant at the time, so instead of following Granny down the lane, she went down to her parents' house and found her brother sitting in their living room.

"Granny's down there by the oil tanks. I think her cows are out. Can you go help her?"

Her brother gave her a smirk and said, "Funny, Sheila."

"What do you mean?"

"They found Granny Schnautz dead in her house the other day. There's no way you saw her."

Sheila never believed in ghosts before she had that experience, but she knew what she saw. "There was no way that wasn't Granny Schnautz," she said.

The house burned down years ago, leaving nothing but a barn behind to mark the location. It makes me curious if Granny is still out there searching for her cows or if she's finally moved on.

DEPOT DINER

232 South Main Street
Griffin, Indiana

In the early evening of March 18, 1925, an F-5 tornado swept through three states, killing 747 people and injuring an additional 2,298. The Tri-State Tornado, as it came to be known, is still listed as the deadliest tornado in U.S. history. The tornado was on the ground for 219 miles as it cut a swatch through Missouri, Illinois and Indiana, leaving a wake of destruction behind it.

Early warning systems weren't as advanced as they are today. Weatherwise farmers knew what to look for, but this one didn't have the same hallmarks as a traditional tornado. Witnesses describe it as a rolling fog, perhaps camouflaged by the debris and soil from the fields.

Entire towns were destroyed, including Griffin, Indiana. Prior to the tornado, Griffin was a thriving farming community with five hundred residents. March would have been a time when farmers were preparing to plant their crops for the year, but that plan was swiftly ruined.

As the tornado bore down on them, residents had very little warning. The skies suddenly darkened, and softball-sized hail pummeled the land, sending people running for cover. One group of people ran into the local general store and sought shelter in the basement, but it wouldn't end up being a safe place. The building collapsed on top of them and then caught on fire, trapping them in the basement to be burned alive.

The tragedies were endless. School had just let out fifteen minutes before the tornado struck. A horse-drawn wagon carrying twenty-five students was

The Depot Diner, current day.

caught by the tornado and sent the children flying out onto the road. The horse and driver were killed immediately, along with three of the children. Another ten died of their injuries later. One boy who survived the impact ran six miles to the neighboring town of New Harmony for help, bringing back doctors to attend to the wounded.

In the aftermath of the tornado, only one building in the small town was untouched. The rest of the town was completely destroyed. Homes, businesses, churches and the school were reduced to toothpicks. In the end, seventy-six people in Griffin lost their lives, with hundreds more suffering injuries.

Surrounding towns, along with the National Guard and Red Cross, came to their aid, but Mother Nature wasn't finished with them. Heavy rains came the day after the tornado, causing the nearby Wabash River to flood its banks. The only way into the town was by boat or on the railway. The National Guard and the American Red Cross rushed to the town, removing the deceased via flatbed rail cars, and attended to the injured, setting up emergency tents for the survivors.

By the following year, the town was slowly rebuilding, but it would never truly be the same again. It's not surprising that several areas in town are haunted.

One story follows the heartache of a woman who lost her baby during the tornado. On quiet, moonless nights, you might hear the sound of her crying as she wanders the streets searching for her baby. The sound starts softly, echoing like wind wailing through the trees, until it morphs into a desperate howl. Sometimes people will also hear a baby crying, making me wonder if the baby is also looking for the mother. Several others have reported seeing her misty apparition floating down the street.

The Tri-State Tornado sign.

Another location with a haunting is the Depot Diner. The building is an authentic train depot building that once sat down the street near the train tracks. In the 1970s, a businessman moved it to its current location and turned it into a restaurant.

In its early days, the diner offered only window service. People could come up and order food and then eat it on the picnic tables out front. Later, a dining room was added to provide more space, and the depot was able to offer indoor seating. It is currently a full-service diner, offering breakfast, lunch and dinner.

I discovered the diner shortly after I moved to the area in 2016. As a medium, I walked inside and immediately picked up on the haunting. There were several ghosts, but the strongest one was an older man. I could all but see him sitting at the table beside me, drinking coffee and enjoying his morning.

I didn't ask about the haunting while I was there. Several years passed before I ran into Michele Simmons Wilkerson, who filled me in on the spooky events that transpired there. You might recognize her name from the haunting at Ziggy's. When I interviewed her about the diner, she stunned me by also sharing stories about her time at the Playhouse. It proves a point to me that some people are predisposed to experiencing hauntings.

Michele owned the Depot Diner for eleven years and felt the haunting immediately. Having several paranormal experiences in her youth, she knew what to look for. When she was a child, her grandmother lived next door to her parents' house. Several of her cousins lived with her grandmother, and the group of children would hang out together. Every Saturday, Michele's mom and grandma would go shopping. While they were gone, the kids often saw a man standing outside the house, usually leaning against a tree.

He was a big man and was dressed like a cowboy, from the cowboy hat on his head to the spurs on his boots. The only thing that set him apart from a living man was the fact that he was gray. There wasn't a trace of color on him. He looked like a newspaper photo as he stood there staring menacingly at the children. Some of the older kids would grab butcher knives, thinking the knives would protect them from the evil apparition. The others, Michele included, knew that knives wouldn't help them in this situation. Eventually, the man would turn and walk through the winterberry bushes and disappear.

Michelle wasn't thinking about ghosts when she took over the Griffin Diner, but it wasn't long before she began experiencing strange phenomena. While the entire building seemed to be haunted, the basement was the one place she tried to avoid at all costs. That was where a scary male ghost lurked. While she never actually saw him, she could feel him without question. She hated going down there. The sensation was so strong, it instantly instilled a fight-or-flight sensation. "You could feel the depression when you walked down the stairs. It was like someone was watching you," she said. Everyone who worked there also felt it. They made a point of rushing to grab what they needed and hurrying back out.

"The hair on the back of your neck stands up, and you just want to run. When you go to leave, they rush you. I'd run up the stairs, and it wouldn't go any farther," she said. It was as though the ghost was trapped in the basement.

One of the waitresses who worked there also experienced the paranormal activity. Becky had worked for the previous owners for eighteen years before Michele bought the diner, so she was well acquainted with the haunting.

Michele would arrive at five o'clock in the morning, but Becky wouldn't get there until six, leaving Michele alone in the building for an hour every morning. Michele immediately headed to the kitchen to begin the food preparation for the day. As she began chopping and dicing ingredients for

The Depot Diner.

the daily specials, she'd often hear the front door open. The sound was soon followed by the clinking of the coffeepots and the scud of a chair being pulled out from one of the tables.

The first time she heard it, she thought she must have forgotten to lock the front door and one of the regulars came in and helped himself to a cup of coffee. As she rushed out of the kitchen, she was stunned to discover that the dining room was empty and the door was firmly locked.

They had several security cameras set up around the diner with a monitor in the kitchen to allow them a view of the dining room. Sometimes, when she would hear the door open, she would look up at the monitor and see the shadowy shape of a person moving through the room. Other times, she'd see floating balls of light dancing through the room. After a few seconds, the screen would turn to static. She'd unplug it and reboot it. When it came back on, everything would be normal again.

If that wasn't creepy enough, Michele actually saw the man several times. She would only catch a quick glimpse of him before he dissipated. "He was an older man, maybe in his sixties. He had gray hair and was a little overweight," she said. She thought he was wearing a flannel shirt, but she doesn't recall what color it was. She didn't stand there long enough to figure it out. She ran outside and waited for Becky to arrive.

Michele didn't recognize the man. He wasn't one of her regular customers. She thought he might have been one of the original owners, but she wasn't sure. She only knew that he showed up every morning for his cup of coffee.

Sometimes she would come in and the energy just felt different. "It felt off. I can't explain it, but it didn't feel good," she said.

"I know you're here," she'd say aloud. If the vibe didn't fade, she'd wait outside for Becky to arrive.

There was often a reason behind the negative vibe. The ghost wasn't friendly. On several occasions, he startled Michele by throwing things at her. "We had a big ice machine that used to sit at the end of the register. We had a big scoop that we used when we needed to fill up buckets. It normally sat on top of the ice machine, pushed toward the back," she said. On several occasions, the metal scoop launched itself across the room, landing near the coffee station with a clank, startling her.

Another place in the diner that she tried to avoid in the mornings was the bathroom. While she was in there, she would hear full-blown conversations. It sounded like people were in the diner talking, but when she'd open the door, the building was completely empty. She also heard the voices when she was in the basement.

Other people experienced the haunting too. "Sometimes people would call me at night and tell me there was someone standing in the window of the diner," she said. Michele and her boyfriend would go check it out but never found anything amiss.

The ghost also liked to move objects. "You could walk through there and set something down on the counter, and it would disappear," she said. They'd search the entire building but never find it again. "It was just gone," she said.

It wasn't long before she began wondering if the ghost from the diner had followed her home. She started hearing strange sounds and got the same negative vibe she felt at the diner. Her boyfriend worked nights, so she would leave the bedroom lights on all night, often sitting up and waiting for him to get home. Some mornings she would wake up with marks on her body.

Becky and her sister, who also worked at the diner, experienced shared encounters. One night they were on the phone and their ears began burning. It was as though the phone became as hot as lava. The next morning, both of them had red ears, as though they'd been burned.

Michele called the pastor from her church. He blessed several prayer cloths and gave them to her, instructing her to place them at the four corners of her house. He also arranged for a group of women to do a cleansing. After they were finished, everything felt better. "It was like walking into a different house. It even smelled different," she said.

Even though the haunting had disappeared from her home, it wasn't gone from the diner. One morning, she walked in to discover the smell of gas. Someone had turned the gas to the oven on during the night. She stood there for a second, trying to gather her bearings, when she felt a rush of wind blow through her, accompanied by a high-pitched scream. The ear-piercing sound grew louder and louder until it finally disappeared, along with the wind. She quickly turned off the gas and aired out the building. "Everything was just bad at that point," she said.

Knowing Michele grew up in Griffin, I asked her if she had ever experienced anything else around town. "There are definitely a few areas in town," she said. "You just feel eyes on you when you're there."

Having spent some time in Griffin, I tend to agree with her. After suffering through such a horrendous tragedy, it stands to reason that the entire town might be haunted.

If you visit Griffin, make sure you check out the Mount Pleasant Cemetery, where many of the victims of the tornado are buried. It's a beautiful place with an overwhelming sense of serenity and grace.

THE HAUNTING IN SAVAH

Savah, Indiana

S avah is the kind of community that feels one way during the light of day but quite another way once the sun sinks below the horizon. The area is known for its lowlands due to its proximity to the Wabash River. It's a place where the sky feels enormous, pressing down on the flat ribbon of land below it. Farm fields stretch like a patchwork quilt in every direction with a sprinkling of houses that are sometimes miles apart. It's an easy place to get lost. Every road looks just like the last, with few identifiable landmarks. Without GPS, you might spend hours trying to find your way out.

I grew up hearing stories about Savah. My stepfather, Doug York, lived there as a child back in the 1950s. He always described the area as a poor, rural community with deep roots. People looked out for one another and lent a hand when one was needed. He said it was the greatest place on earth to be a kid.

His family was dirt poor, but so was everyone else. They spent the summer fishing at the Wabash River and playing ball at the school. None of those things required money.

It's possible that Doug descended from some of the first settlers to the area. In 1807, the first child was born in the area that would later become Mount Vernon. Her name was Malinda Weir. After she grew up, she married into the York family, and they moved to Savah.

Savah has a desolate vibe to it at first glance. It's all sky.

I never wondered about Savah being haunted until I began asking questions. As it turns out, there seems to be a ghost or two lurking around every corner.

I found out about the ghost stories after chatting with a young woman named Bailey Stewart. If you met her, you'd swear she was still in high school, but she's actually much older and is the mother of two children. She invited me to join her and her sister, Josie, at her grandmother's house. She said her grandma had ghost stories she was eager to share, and that was all it took to lure me out into the cold day.

If I was expecting Bailey's grandmother to be a frail, white-haired grandma, I was sorely mistaken. She's so far from frail; the two versions are in separate zip codes. Sue Aldrich is a dynamo.

My friend Traci Hoehn went with me to meet with her. When we pulled up, a big friendly Dalmatian named Sarge bounded out to greet us. Sue was at the door to welcome us in. "Don't worry, he's friendly!" she called out, smiling.

Her sprawling ranch-style home was filled with memories from her decades of keeping and showing horses. Tall, shiny trophies line one bookcase, with horse art hanging on every wall. Even her claw-foot bathtub was hand-painted with the likeness of some of her favorite horses.

Sue has lived in Savah for more than forty years after marrying her husband, Spencer, whose family has been there for generations.

We sat down at her kitchen island, and she began telling us ghost stories from the past. The first involved a house that is no longer standing. It was formerly located on a lot beside the church. "It was a really odd house," she told us. "There was a secret passage that led up to the bedroom. I never saw it, but I heard about it." She went on to tell us that her daughter, Andrea, who is Bailey's mother, spent a lot of time there as a teenager. Andrea's friend lived in the house, so she would visit frequently, but the house always gave her chills. Odd things happened from time to time. They'd hear footsteps in empty rooms and the sounds of doors creaking open when no one else was in the house.

When Andrea went to sleep some nights, she would feel the covers shift on the bed. She'd hold herself as still as possible, not even daring to breathe. Her mind raced. Had the covers shifted, or did someone move them? Most nights the sensation only happened once, but some nights it didn't stop there. She'd lay there, praying for it to end. An eternity would pass as though the ghost was biding his time, waiting for the perfect opportunity to pounce. Then, she'd feel the distinct sensation of someone running a finger down the bottom of her foot. It happened more than once. Each time it did, she'd launch herself out of bed, looking around the room with wide eyes. It was one thing to feel the covers move because she could rationalize it as gravity pulling them to the floor, but the sensation on her foot was very real. There was no way gravity tickled her feet.

Andrea was already on the brink of terror when something happened that would send her fleeing from the house. One night, she was sitting in bed talking to her friend when a bedside lamp levitated off the table and slammed to the ground. They both stared wide-eyed. There was no way they had imagined that. They climbed through the hidden door and made their way downstairs and out of the house. It was the last night she would spend there.

The house burned down years ago, leaving nothing more than a memory.

Sue wasn't finished with her ghost stories though. She leaned back in her chair as Sarge walked over. He rested his big, spotted muzzle on her leg and looked up at her with adoring eyes.

"I should probably tell you about Spencer's family house, too," she said, stroking the dog's head.

Bailey had already filled me in about the house. She called it the "American Pickers" house because it was once filled to the brim with antiques and other interesting collectibles. "Great-grandma was a bit of a hoarder," she said with a laugh.

"I've gotten everything out of there that was of value," Sue said. "All that's left is junk. The house is pretty much held together by the grace of God and coon poop," she said, causing us all to laugh.

And then she uttered the words I dreamt of hearing: "Do you want to see it?"

I was beside myself with excitement. As someone who has turned ghosts into a profession, getting to walk into an old haunted house is the absolute foundation of my fantasies.

The old house was only a five-minute drive from their house, bringing us past wide-open, wintering fields and flat gray skies. In the summer, the fields would be filled with soybeans and corn, transforming the pale ground into a green wonderland topped by cerulean blue skies. Today, it just looked foreboding and desolate.

When Sue and Spencer were first married, his grandmother still lived there. She had moved some of her belongings into a mobile home that sat next to the house and left the house empty for reasons I can only imagine. Had she also felt the ghosts? It wasn't something most people talked about back then, but Sue was fairly certain something or someone was still there.

"I have felt Spencer's grandfather in the house, but not his grandmother. She always came to me in the barn." She then went on to tell me about his grandmother. She described her as being petite and kind with an absolute love for horses. Her name was Ina, but everyone called her Inie.

We pulled up to the property, and I was all eyes, trying to take it all in. The house was exactly as she described it. One good gust of wind could have taken it down.

"Let's start with the barn," she said, walking past the house toward a large red barn. It was the kind of barn you see less and less as the decades pass. When they weather and fall down, they are often replaced with metal counterparts. Much to my dismay, the era of big red barns is quickly coming to an end.

The old barn.

We reached the barn and climbed a big step to get inside. Sue led us to the tack room where they once kept the saddles and harnesses for the horses.

"We broke Grandma Inie's heart when we fixed the gate to the barn," she said and then told us the rest of the story.

When Sue and Spencer would go out each evening to feed and water their horses, they'd often find the door to the tack room wide open. Because they sometimes kept bags of seed there and didn't want the horses to have access to them, they always made sure the door was locked. After finding it open a few times, Spencer chided Sue about it, telling her she needed to be more careful. Sue was fairly certain she was being careful, but she didn't argue.

One evening, they came out to the barn and, once again, found the door to the tack room wide open. Sue quickly closed and locked it before Spencer could see it and then hurried to the hayloft ladder. She was only several rungs up when she heard the sound of someone yelling. She ran back and opened the door, only to find Spencer's Grandma Inie standing there.

The mystery of the open door was now solved. Inie loved going in and looking at all the old tack and was sneaking in there when no one was looking. Spencer fixed the gate and put an end to her shenanigans, which broke her heart.

Even though they don't use the barn for their own horses any longer, Sue still sometimes goes out there. She almost always feels Grandma Inie's presence. Sometimes, she even finds the tack room door open.

"Want to check out the house?" she asked.

She didn't have to ask twice. We followed her back to the old house, which I later found out was Savah's first schoolhouse. When the current school, which is now the community center, was built, they moved the house down the road to where it currently stands.

Sue unlocked the door for us, and we picked our way into the house. Time hadn't been kind to the old home. The floors were spongy, and the walls looked as though they were ready to fall at any given moment. Old wallpaper covered every wall, most of it ripped and rotten but still showing the beautiful details of a bygone era.

As we stood there, my ears began ringing. Using it as a gateway to my abilities, I tuned into the sound and quickly pulled in more information.

"There's a younger woman here," I told them.

I began seeing her in my mind's eye. She was in her twenties or possibly thirties. She was dressed in a pink slip with thin straps and had long, wild red hair. I described her to the group, but no one recognized her. Spencer's grandmother had curly black hair, so it wasn't her.

"Has anything strange ever happened to you here?" I asked.

Sue gave me a wry smile. "Only one thing, and it's pretty funny," she said. Her granddaughters started laughing, so I knew it was going to be a good story.

"We kept some of our horses here, so we had to come out every day to feed and water them. One evening, we showed up right when it was starting to get dark. Spencer was in the barn, but I came into the house to poke around. I looked out the window and saw something odd," she said.

When Spencer finished up, she asked him if his grandpa was stocky and barrel-chested. He looked at her oddly but confirmed what she described.

"Why?" he asked.

"Well, because I just saw him out back taking a pee," she said with a laugh.

What she saw was startling but humorous. Spencer's grandparents didn't have running water or indoor plumbing when they lived in the house. They had an outhouse and a well, but Spencer's grandfather often just used the backyard when nature called. Apparently, he still did it in his afterlife.

"Welcome to Savah! We've got it all!" Sue said with a laugh. "You know how men turn their back and they have 'the stance.' I just assumed that's what it was."

Since we were close, Sue brought us over to the Bethesda General Baptist Church. Bailey always felt a sense of unease in the basement and wanted to see if I was able to pick up anything.

My stepfather, Doug, told me a few stories about the old church. He went there as a child and said there were two doors on the front of the church. Back in the old days, the men walked through one door and the women

The Bethesda General Baptist Church.

walked through the other. He said there used to be a rail running down the middle of the aisle to keep them further separated.

We walked into the church and checked it out. It's been my experience that most churches are haunted. As you read this, I'm assuming some of you just rolled your eyes, but it's true. At the time of death, many people don't cross over into heaven because they're fearful about the misdeeds they did when they were alive. What better place to go for possible salvation than a church?

I definitely felt the presence of ghosts in the church but didn't bother to tune into any of them. They were obviously there for a purpose, and I didn't want to disrupt them. We then headed down into the basement. The room is long and rectangular. It struck me as the kind of room where the church might have potluck dinners or offer Sunday school classes for the younger members.

I found myself instantly drawn to a small bathroom at the far end of the room. It hadn't been used in a long time and had become a small storage room, but the vibe was strong. There was definitely something in there, and it was a bit agitated.

"The kids called him Black Jack," Bailey told me. Apparently, she wasn't the only one who felt him over the years.

I was also told that kids used to dare each other to go into the church basement at night to see if they saw him. Overseers of the church eventually began locking the church doors to prevent the nighttime escapades.

We didn't stay long. I turned on my spirit box for a few minutes to see if anyone wanted to talk to us, but no voices came through, so we shut it down and left.

We drove by the Savah Community Center. I can remember going there as a child for family gatherings. At one point, it was the community school. I'm sure ghosts from the past remain there, but the doors were locked.

The last place on our list was Sue's house.

It didn't surprise me that Sue had ghosts. I believe that mediumship abilities usually run in families, often being passed down from mother to daughter. Both Bailey and Sue had shared stories with me about incidents when they sensed a ghostly presence. It might surprise them to know they are gifted with a sixth sense. Most people don't feel ghosts.

Bailey was always close to her great-grandmother on her mother's side, whom she called Granny. When Granny was dying, she told Bailey to not worry about having children. Bailey had endometriosis, and it had been a concern. Granny also stunned her by telling her that she would have a son instead of a daughter.

The Savah Community Center was once the school but is now used for community activities and meetings.

After Granny died, Bailey went into labor on Granny's birthday and delivered a healthy baby boy, just like Granny predicted. A few nights after she came home from the hospital, she had a dream about Granny. In the dream, Granny was yelling at her to wake up. "Get up!" she yelled, pulling Bailey from sleep. As she opened her eyes, she saw Granny standing beside her bed. Granny pointed toward the baby bed. Bailey raced to the bed to find her newborn son choking on embryonic fluid. She scooped him up, and he coughed up the liquid. Granny had saved her son's life.

Once we were back at Sue's house, Bailey told me, "You really need to see the basement." Bailey and Josie felt there was something supernatural going on down there.

Of course, I was game. "Lead the way!" I told them.

I started feeling something almost immediately. It seemed to grow stronger as I walked farther down the hallway. I found myself drawn to one bedroom.

"This is one of the strongest places I feel it!" Bailey said, happy to have her suspicions confirmed.

My friend Traci is also a medium, so I asked her what she felt.

"I feel a young male," she said.

I nodded. My ears were ringing like crazy, so I tuned in and was immediately treated to a photograph in my mind's eye of a young man with brown hair, sitting on a fence. He was wearing a light blue button-down shirt, and he was smiling.

I relayed my impressions to the group. "He's not negative. He might have come with the land," I told them.

Sue then told me that they built the house themselves but that she felt something when they first checked out the property. She also told us there was an old family cemetery just south of the house, so it could have been an old homestead a century ago.

"He doesn't want anything. He's just here." I smiled at Bailey and Josie. "He probably enjoys hanging out with the pretty young girls here."

Both of the women shuddered, which gave me a laugh. No one likes to imagine invisible people watching them. We finished up, and I headed to my car.

I was on my way home before I realized I wasn't alone. There was a ghost in the car.

When my ears ring, the tones are always different. Each ghost has its own tone, and this one was the same one I heard at the old house where Grandma Inie had once lived.

Later, my friend Sandy MacLeod called me, and I asked her to tune in to see if she could confirm my suspicions. Sandy is also a medium and is very good at intuiting from a distance. I've often asked her to tune in while we've been on the phone, and she's provided verifiable information.

"I see her as being in her thirties. She's slim. She was from the 1930s or '40s time period...and she has red hair."

Bingo.

As I went to bed later that night, I could hear her follow me into my bedroom. After I got appropriately snuggled under the covers, I picked up a book, which is part of my bedtime routine, and started reading. All of a sudden, I caught movement out of the corner of my eye. I glanced over just in time to see the misty outline of a woman walk past the foot of my bed.

Most people would find this alarming, but it was just another day in my abnormal life. Hopefully, she will eventually grow bored with me and will find her way back to Inie's house. In the meantime, she hangs over my shoulder, watching as I write about her.

Such is life when it isn't death instead.

CONCLUSION

For every light there is a shadow. And for every shadow, there is darkness. Light can chase away a shadow, but darkness has no power over the light. It loses every single time.

Over the years, I've learned a lot about life by studying death. What I've discovered is fascinating. Paranormal investigating, at least for me, isn't about the thrills and the adrenaline rushes of exploring spooky locations. It isn't about collecting riveting evidence I can show to my friends. It's about people.

Ghosts aren't always the wispy shapes that drift across moonlit cemeteries. They aren't even the apparitions that move through empty rooms, filling the ominous silence with the sound of their phantom footsteps. They are what's left of us.

The noises you hear in your kitchen late at night when you're home alone could be someone's grandma who became confused when she died and didn't cross over into the light. The angry man haunting the basement of a business could be a former owner who lost everything due to a poor decision and is afraid to move on. The items in your house that keep getting knocked to the ground could be due to a child who didn't know where to go when she died one hundred years ago.

A friend of mine was terrified by the strange occurrences that kept happening in his house. The lights would flicker at odd times, and his pets would stare attentively at empty corners. Sometimes, he thought he heard someone calling his name when he was home alone.

It terrified him. He imagined a demon lurking around the corner, intent on stealing his soul. He screamed at empty air, telling the entity to leave him alone, threatening it with violence if it didn't. And then he had a dream.

In the dream, he saw his sister who had passed away a few years ago after dying by suicide. She was sorry for all the turmoil she put the family through, and her soul was tortured.

When he awoke, he realized the haunting he was experiencing wasn't what he thought it was. It wasn't demons or malicious entities. It was the girl he shared a treehouse with and fought over the backseat on long family car rides. Through this knowledge, he was able to talk to her and provide her with the healing she needed to find her way to the light.

I tell you this story because too many people label every haunting as being something evil. Most of the time, it isn't. All it takes is a little light to chase away the shadows.

Be the light in your world. Be the one who brightens a room instead of darkening it. And if you encounter something unexplainable, realize it might not be what you think it is.

The next time you visit a haunted location, remind yourself that it might have once been someone's home, and for the ghosts, it still is.

RESOURCES

Mount Vernon

County Infirmary: The Posey 1, no. 4 (October 1995). Newsletter of the Posey Historical Society.

Criswell, Wally. "New Albany–Built Eclipse Made History with Her Fast Run from New Orleans." floydlibrary.org/wp-content/uploads/2016/07/eclipseandshipbuilding.pdf.

Find-A-Grave. "Poor Infirmary Cemetery." www.findagrave.com/cemetery/2550171/poor-infirmary-cemetery.

Historical Marker Database. "Posey County History/Early Mt. Vernon History." www.hmdb.org/m.asp?m=48215.

"Mt. Vernon—County Seat of Posey County, Indiana." ingenweb.org/inposey/towns/mtVernon.html.

Redwine, James M. *Gavel Gamut Greetings from JPeg Ranch*. Authorhouse, 2009.

———. *Judge Lynch!* Authorhouse, 2008.

Wikipedia. "Mount Vernon, Indiana." en.wikipedia.org/wiki/Mount_Vernon,_Indiana.

Keck Motor Building

Norbeck, Jack C. "Keck-Gonnerman Steam Engine History." Farm Collector. www.farmcollector.com/steam-traction/keck-gonnerman-steam-engine-history.

New Harmony

De Wolfe, Elizabeth A., ed. *American Communal Societies Series Number Four*. University of New England, n.d.

English, Eileen Aiken, comp. *Demographic Directory of the Harmony Society*. N.d.

Lockridge, Ross F. *The Old Fauntleroy Home*. Published for the New Harmony Memorial Commission courtesy of Mrs. Edmund Burke Ball, 1939.

Owen, Jane Blaffer. *New Harmony, Indiana: Like a River, Not a Lake*. Bloomington: Indiana University Press, 2015.

Poseyville

Facebook. "History of Poseyville, Indiana." www.facebook.com/ PoseyvilleHistory/posts/i-managed-to-find-a-series-of-history-articles-in-the-posey-county-news-in-1975-/1467729030218205.

Philibert-Ortega, Gena. "Carnegie Libraries: A History of Library Philanthropy from Steel." Genealogy Bank. blog.genealogybank. com/carnegie-libraries-a-history-of-library-philanthropy-from-steel. html?https://www.genealogybank.com/static/lp/2014/nov/obits.html &gclid=CjwKCAjw3riIBhAwEiwAzD3Tie-4mltsLKKjXOfV5Zq25U84 V7GwwbjVhUyIxgK5RibfPfURTV4mzxoCM-IQAvD_BwE.

"Poseyville Carnegie Public Library." sites.google.com/site/ indianascarnegielibraries/indiana-s-carnegie-libraries/poseyville-1904.

Greathouse School

Wikipedia. "Point Township, Posey County, Indiana." en.wikipedia.org/ wiki/Point_Township,_Posey_County,_Indiana.

Griffin

Wikipedia. "Tri-State Tornado Outbreak." en.wikipedia.org/wiki/Tri-State_tornado_outbreak.

YouTube. "The Story of the Griffin Tornado." www.youtube.com/ watch?v=DTRdxFksk_g.

Savah

HomeTown Locator. "Savah (in Posey County, IN) Populated Place Profile." indiana.hometownlocator.com/in/posey/savah.cfm.

ABOUT THE AUTHOR

Joni Mayhan is a seasoned paranormal investigator and the author of numerous paranormal books, something that often leads her into dark places that others avoid. To learn more about her, check out her website, Jonimayhan.com.

Also by Joni Mayhan

True Paranormal Nonfiction
When Ghosts Are Near
Hanover Haunting: The DeAnna Simpson Story
Haunted New Harmony
Ghost Magnet
Spirit Nudges: Allowing Help from the Other Side
Signs of Spirits: When Loved Ones Visit
Ruin of Souls
Dark and Scary Things: A Sensitive's Guide to the Paranormal World
Ghost Voices
Bones in the Basement: Surviving the S.K. Pierce Haunted Victorian Mansion
The Soul Collector
Devil's Toy Box
Ghostly Defenses: A Sensitive's Guide for Protection

Paranormal Fiction
Ember Angels
Crazy Dead People (Shelby and Fugly Paranormal Thriller, Book 1)
Demon Ala Mode (Shelby and Fugly Paranormal Thriller, Book 2)
Lightning Strikes (Angels of Ember Dystopian Trilogy, Book 1)
Ember Rain (Angels of Ember Dystopian Trilogy, Book 2)
Angel Storm (Angels of Ember Dystopian Trilogy, Book 3)
The Spirit Board (Winter Woods, Book 1)
The Labyrinth (Winter Woods, Book 2)
The Corvus (Winter Woods, Book 3)